First Dinosaur Encyclopedia

REVISED EDITION
Assistant editor Debangana Banerjee
Assistant art editor Kartik Gera
Project editor Suneha Dutta
Senior editor Shatarupa Chaudhuri
DTP designer Bimlesh Tiwary
Managing editors Laura Gilbert, Alka Thakur Hazarika
Managing art editors Diane Peyton Jones, Romi Chakraborty
Producer Isobel Comley
Producer, pre-production Nadine King
Publisher Sarah Larter
Publishing director Sophie Mitchell
Art director Stuart Jackman
CTS manager Balwant Singh
Publisher Sarah Larter
Jacket editor Ishani Nandi
Jacket designer Kartik Gera
Consultant John Woodward

ORIGINAL EDITION
Written and edited by Caroline Bingham
Design team Jane Tetzlaff, Tory Gordon-Harris, Clare Harris, Claire Patane, Mary Sandberg, Helen Chapman, Kath Northam
Art editor Rachael Foster
Consultant Dougal Dixon B.SC. (Hons.), M.SC
Publishing Manager Sue Leonard
Jacket Designer Karen Hood
Picture Researcher Liz Moore
Production Controller Lucy Baker
DTP Designer Emma Hansen-Knarhoi
Category Publisher Mary Ling
DK Picture Library Rose Horridge, Claire Bowers

First published in Great Britain in 2007
This paperback edition first published in 2018
by Dorling Kindersley Limited
80 Strand, London, WC2R 0RL

2 4 6 8 10 9 7 5 3 1
001–280450–Aug/2018

A CIP catalogue record for this book is available from the British Library.

ISBN 978-0-2413-7649-2

Printed and bound in India

Contents

Age of the dinosaurs

Let's look at dinosaurs

Triassic dinosaurs

There is a question at the bottom of each page...

Jurassic dinosaurs

Cretaceous dinosaurs

Other forms of life

Fossils

End of the dinosaurs

Reference section

Baby *T. rex* may have been covered in fur.

About this book

The pages of this book have special features that will show you how to get your hands on as much information as possible! Look out for these:

The Picture detective will get you searching through each section for the answers.

Turn and learn tells you where to look for more information on a subject.

Every page is colour-coded to show you which section it is in.

Age of the dinosaurs

The Earth has an incredibly long history, as it formed about 4,600 million years ago. Geologists divide the passage of time since into huge chunks called eras. The giant dinosaurs lived in the Mesozoic Era.

Eoraptor was a Triassic dinosaur.

A question of time

Different dinosaurs lived at different times, and many of the best-known dinosaurs never actually met. For example, no *T. rex* ever tried to kill a *Stegosaurus* because their existence was separated by about 80 million years.

The Mesozoic Era

This era is divided into three time spans, or periods.

The **Cretaceous** period was ruled by an amazing variety of dinosaurs.

The **Jurassic** period saw the emergence of massive plant-eating dinosaurs.

The **Triassic** period, the oldest, saw the appearance of the Earth's first dinosaurs.

Geological time is always shown with the oldest period at the bottom of the list. It reflects the sequence in which rocks are laid down.

Cretaceous: 145 to 66 million years ago

Human beings (*Homo sapiens*) didn't appear until very recently in the Earth's history.

Homo sapiens

Picture detective

Look through the Age of the Dinosaurs pages to identify each of the picture clues below.

Turn and learn
Where *Albertosaurus* roamed:
pp. 68-69

We know a lot about their size and appearance from fossil evidence.

The “terrible lizard”

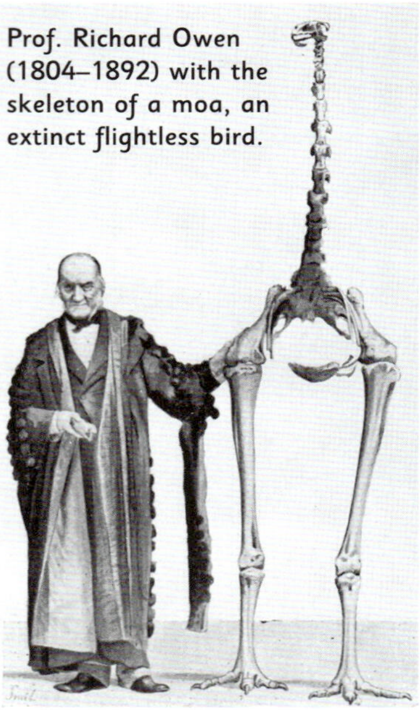

Prof. Richard Owen (1804–1892) with the skeleton of a moa, an extinct flightless bird.

Scientists once believed dinosaur fossils were the bones of a type of lizard. In fact, the word “dinosaur” means “terrible lizard”. It was first used in 1841.

Lizard

A starting point

When Richard Owen first coined the term “dinosaur”, only three of the creatures had been identified: *Iguanodon*, *Megalosaurus*, and *Hylaeosaurus*.

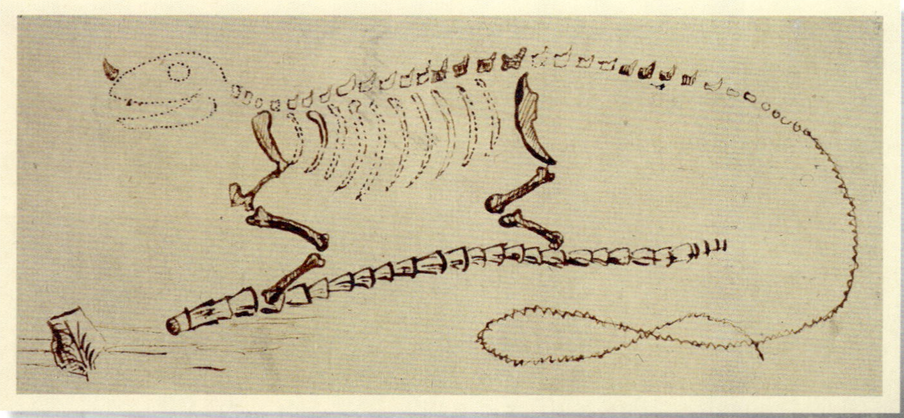

The first sketch of *Iguanodon* had a spike positioned on its snout.

It’s the same one!

Is it two-footed or four? Where does that spikey bit go? Ideas about dinosaurs change over the years, as these portrayals of *Iguanodon* show.

Was *Iguanodon* a plant-eater or a meat-eater?

Where in the world?

From sparse beginnings, dinosaurs have now been found on every continent, including the now frozen Antarctica. This map gives an idea of where just a few dinosaur remains have been found.

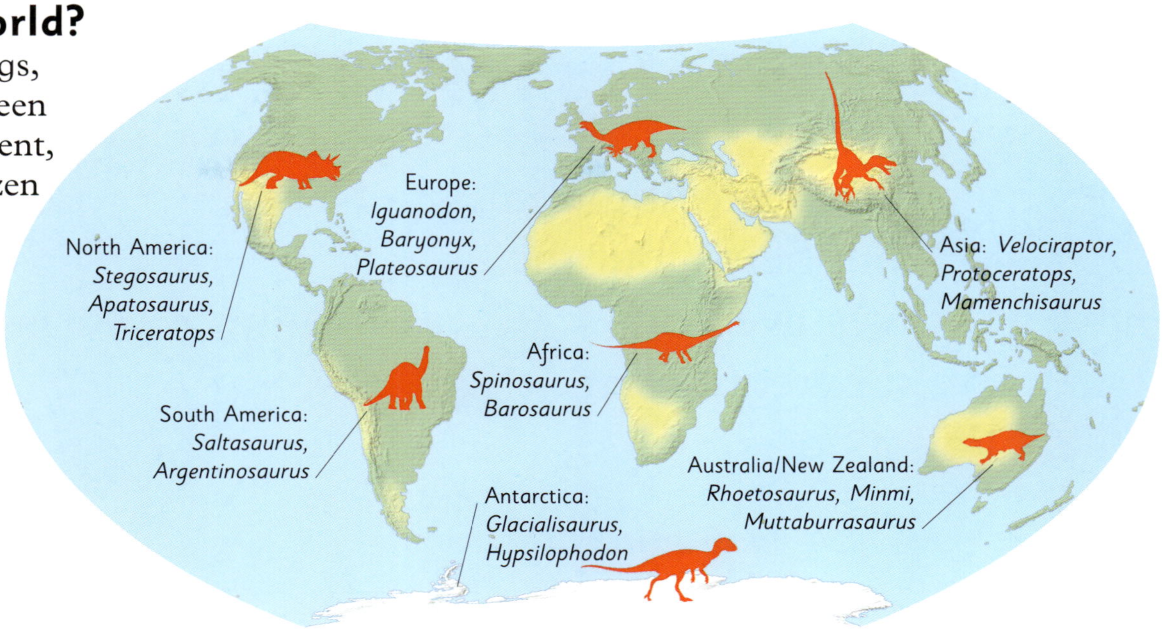

Turn and learn

What a dinosaur is: **pp. 14–15**

In the 1850s, a sculpture of *Iguanodon* showed a lizard crawling on its belly.

The name *Iguanodon* means “iguana toothed”. The teeth were like those of the iguana, the modern, plant-eating lizard.

We now know that *Iguanodon* had spikes on its thumbs, not on its nose.

Scientists believe that *Iguanodon* could walk on four feet, as well as on two.

It was a plant-eater.

A very different Earth

The Earth is constantly changing. Today there are seven continents, but the first dinosaurs lived on one giant supercontinent called Pangaea.

A moving jigsaw

The Earth's crust is made up of sections, called plates, which are always on the move. Continents rest on the plates. Over time, this movement changes the shape of the land.

It's breaking up

During the late Triassic period, Pangaea began to break up to form two supercontinents. By the end of the Cretaceous period, the land masses had undergone huge changes. From space, the Earth would have looked more like it does today, with large continents separated by gigantic oceans.

The Triassic period saw the world's land all joined together as a supercontinent.

What are the names of the Earth's seven continents?

We're free to roam

The existence of one huge land mass meant that, in the early to mid-Triassic period, animals and plants were similar throughout the world.

What was different?

Pangaea's world had no ice caps and the land was hot and dry; large areas of desert dominated the centre of this vast continent.

Pangaea means "All Earth".

Jurassic period

The land mass split apart in the Jurassic period, forming two huge continents.

Cretaceous period

The land masses we know today began to appear during the Cretaceous period.

Africa, Asia, Australia, Antarctica, North America, South America, and Europe.

What did they see?

The dinosaurs looked out onto a very different world from the one we see today. It was a world without roads, houses, parks, and all the machines humans use. So what was it like?

Habitat

Like us, the dinosaurs lived in different habitats. A habitat is an area that animals and plants share. It may be a desert, or a busy city street.

Iguanodon was a plant-eater. By the time *Iguanodon* lived, the first flowering plants had appeared.

How many different types of grass are there today?

Triassic scene

From Triassic forests...

The first dinosaurs saw only brown and green plants – there were no flowers. Giant forests contained trees that were similar to plants we know today, only larger.

Cycad

Ginkgo leaves

Monkey puzzle

Horsetail

... to Cretaceous flowers

The first flowering plants, such as magnolias and passion flowers, appeared in the Cretaceous period. By the late Cretaceous, there were also buttercups.

Magnolia

Fossilized dinosaur dung (coprolite)

Fossilized grass remains were found in dinosaur dung.

What about grass?

Until recently, scientists believed grass evolved after the dinosaurs, but there's now proof that some dinosaurs did eat grass. And it may have been grass that was several metres tall!

Dinosaur habitats

The dinosaurs enjoyed a huge variety of habitats, including those below.

Large areas of **desert** were common in the Mesozoic Era.

Trees in Triassic **forests** were protected from over-browsing by tough needles.

Mountains increasingly appeared in the Mesozoic Era.

Scrublands were huge areas of scrubby, drought-resistant plants.

Cretaceous **swamps** were good places for fossil preservation.

Triassic dinosaurs stayed close to coasts or **riverbanks**.

Buttercup

There are about 10,000 different types.

Let's look at dinosaurs

Large... small... meat-eater... plant-eater... There was an incredible variety of dinosaurs and we will probably never know just how many different kinds there were.

Sauropods, such as *Barosaurus*, were the largest land animals ever.

T. rex was a large theropod.

The very first dinosaurs, such as *Lesothosaurus*, were all small. Larger dinosaurs, such as *Stegosaurus*, came later.

I've got that!

Dinosaurs had plenty of features in common.

Scaly skin, and feathers in some cases, covered the bodies of dinosaurs.

Long tails were used for balance and as a whip to fight off enemies.

Legs were held straight under the body.

Whether meat-eater (theropod) or plant-eater (sauropod), all had **claws**.

How long did dinosaurs live?

How many dinosaurs?

Scientists think there may have been at least 1,500 different dinosaur types, and probably many more. We know of about 800 that can be confirmed as distinct types, so there are a lot more to discover.

Pentaceratops means "five-horned face".

How are they named?

Dinosaurs are usually named after the person who found them, after their features, or after the place they were found.

Picture detective

Look through the Let's Look at Dinosaurs pages to identify each of the picture clues below.

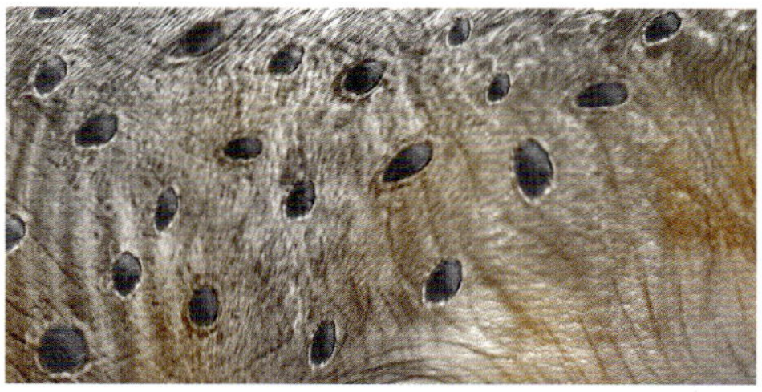

Turn and learn

T. rex: **pp. 76-77**
Triceratops: **pp. 72-73**

Nobody knows. Some may have lived for 80 years.

What is a dinosaur?

Two legs or four? Meat-eater or plant-eater? What made a dinosaur? They all had four limbs, though many walked on two. There were a number of other features they had in common.

Long tails

Scientists believe dinosaurs held their tails above the ground as there is no evidence of drag marks where trackways have been found.

Meat-eating dinosaurs, such as *Giganotosaurus*, were known as theropods.

Scaly skin

Impressions of dinosaur skin are rare, but palaeontologists have found enough to know that many dinosaurs had scaly skin, rather like lizards today.

Cold-blooded lizards have to warm up in sunlight; they cannot control their temperature.

Were dinosaurs warm-blooded?

It's likely that the meat-eating dinosaurs were warm-blooded, like us, but scientists are not sure if the biggest plant-eaters were, too. Warm-blooded animals use food as fuel to stay warm, so the giant plant-eaters may not have managed to eat enough to do this.

Giganotosaurus skulls had huge "windows".

Skull holes

Dinosaur skulls had large holes, or "windows". These made them lighter, which was necessary as some of the largest skulls were almost as long as a car.

Meat-eaters had sharp claws.

Plant-eaters had blunt toenails.

Clue in the claws

Meat-eating dinosaurs were known as theropods, which means "beast-footed", because they had sharp, hooked claws on their toes. Plant-eating dinosaurs (sauropods) tended to have blunt hooves or toenails.

Egg layers

All dinosaurs laid eggs – some in nests, just as birds do today. The baby developed in the egg until it was ready to hatch. About 40 kinds of dinosaur eggs have been discovered.

Walking tall

Dinosaurs walked on their toes with their legs directly under their bodies.

Dinosaurs walked on upright, pillar-like legs.

Crocodiles stand with their knees and elbows slightly bent.

Lizards sprawl, with their knees and elbows held at right angles to their bodies.

A hip question

Dinosaurs can be split into two groups, according to their hip bones: the saurischians (lizard-hipped) and the ornithischians (bird-hipped).

T. rex

weird or what?

Strangely enough, scientists believe that birds have evolved from lizard-hipped dinosaurs – not bird-hipped dinosaurs as you might expect!

Saurischians

All meat-eating dinosaurs were lizard-hipped, but some plant-eaters were also lizard-hipped. *T. rex* was lizard-hipped, but so was the mighty plant-eating *Diplodocus*, whom you will meet on page 50.

I'm in this group!

Saurischians can be divided into two main groups.

Theropods, the meat-eaters, such as *Dilophosaurus*.

Sauropodomorphs, such as *Brachiosaurus*, with their small heads and long necks.

Triceratops

Ornithischians

These were all plant-eaters. The swept-back bones allowed more room for the digestive organs, and meant their bellies could be carried well back. This made them more stable, and allowed some to walk or run away from danger on two legs.

I'm in that group!

Ornithischians can be divided into three main groups.

Thyreophorans, the four-footed, armour-plated dinosaurs (e.g. *Stegosaurus*).

Marginocephalians, who had heads with bony frills or horns (e.g. *Triceratops*).

Ornithopods, the two-legged plant-eaters (e.g. *Iguanodon*).

From little to big

Not all dinosaurs were giants, as is often believed. The smaller dinosaurs, such as *Oviraptor*, would have barely reached up to the large plant-eaters' ankles!

Long in the tooth?

Like humans, most dinosaurs had teeth.

Human molars are used for grinding food before it is swallowed.

Ankylosaurs had small, ridged teeth for slicing up plant matter.

Sauropods had long, peg-like teeth.

Thigh bone from a *Brachiosaurus*

From small...

Some dinosaurs are best described as tiny, such as the rabbit-sized *Micropachycephalosaurus*. Its lengthy name means "tiny, thick-headed lizard".

Micropachycephalosaurus

... to dog-sized...

The meat-eating *Oviraptor* was about 2 m (6.5 ft) from snout to tail. This dinosaur had an oddly shaped toothless beak.

Oviraptor lived in the Gobi Desert in Mongolia about 80 million years ago.

Big head

It's difficult to imagine how large dinosaurs grew. Just look at this picture of a fossilized skull from a dinosaur that roamed the Sahara Desert 90 million years ago.

Carcharodontosaurus skull from the mid-Cretaceous period

Antarctosaurus

Turn and learn

Oviraptor: **p. 23**
Sauropods: **pp. 50–53**

Antarctosaurus had an immensely long neck, which helped it to feed high in the treetops.

... to truck-sized

The large plant-eaters, the sauropods, were massive. *Antarctosaurus* was about 18 m (59 ft) long and would have towered over you. Other plant-eaters may have been larger still. Experts believe that large sauropods ate enough plants every day to equal the weight of a small car.

Find a friend

Many male animals today compete to win a mate. Stags crash their antlers together, while birds display colourful feathers. Scientists believe dinosaurs had to compete in similar ways.

How did they court?

Dinosaurs may have used their head crests to show off, just like a peacock uses its colourful tail feathers.

Corythosaurus

Courtship displays tell females which males are strong and likely to make healthy young.

Peacock

Pachycephalosaurus

This dinosaur had bony spikes on its head and snout.

Bone head

Pachycephalosaurus's head was 80 cm (2.5 ft) long. The dome was made of solid bone as thick as a bowling ball.

Pachycephalosaurus skull

Fighting fit

During the breeding season, male *Pachycephalosaurus* may have butted each other in fights over females. Their thick skulls could have absorbed the impacts.

Did they talk?

Nobody knows if dinosaurs made sounds, but we suspect they did. *Parasaurolophus,* a hadrosaur (a duck-billed dinosaur), may have done this by blowing air through its crest.

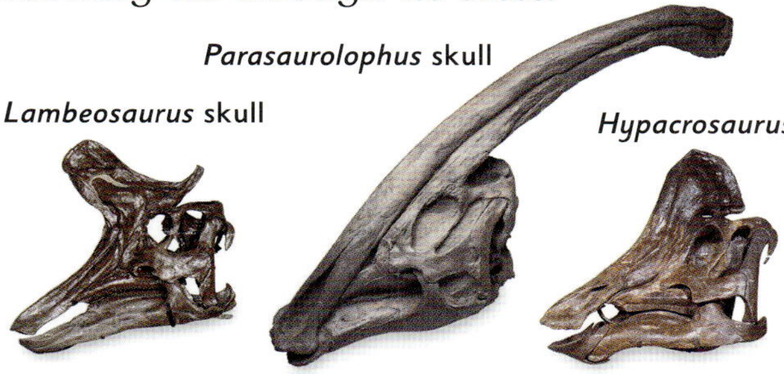

Other hadrosaurs had different-shaped crests, suggesting they made different sounds.

Turn and learn
Crested hadrosaurs: **pp. 70–71**

Parasaurolophus

Brachylophosaurus

Talk like a frog

Brachylophosaurus had a short, solid crest. It may have had an inflatable pouch on the outside of this that could be used to make noises, a bit like a frog's throat pouch.

In the forests of North America.

Extraordinary eggs!

Scientists have been lucky enough to find lots of fossilized dinosaur eggs, and even nests. There is a huge variety of sizes and shapes – from small, circular eggs that would fit into the palm of your hand, to eggs the size of cannonballs.

Large scale

This massive egg was found in China and is thought to have been laid by a *Therizinosaurus*. There were larger eggs – the largest was laid by a dinosaur called *Macroelongatoolithus*.

This dinosaur egg fossil is from Mongolia.

A muddy home

Some eggs were laid in mud, which proved a perfect base for fossilization. These are *Maiasaura* eggs from Montana, USA.

Many shapes

Some dinosaur eggs were round, but others were elongated, rather like a loaf of bread.

This is a hen's egg. It shows just how large the *Therizinosaurus* egg was.

Oviraptor nest from China, showing the eggs laid in a spiral pattern. Each egg is approximately 16 cm (6 in) long.

Were dinosaur egg shells soft and leathery like those of snakes?

I'm making a break for it!

A tiny dinosaur hatchling would break out of its egg casing. While some dinosaurs were probably ready to look after themselves after hatching, others would have depended on parental help for food and protection.

Egg care?

Did dinosaurs sit on their eggs, like birds today? Some did; this *Citipati* died and was fossilized sitting on her eggs some 80 million years ago.

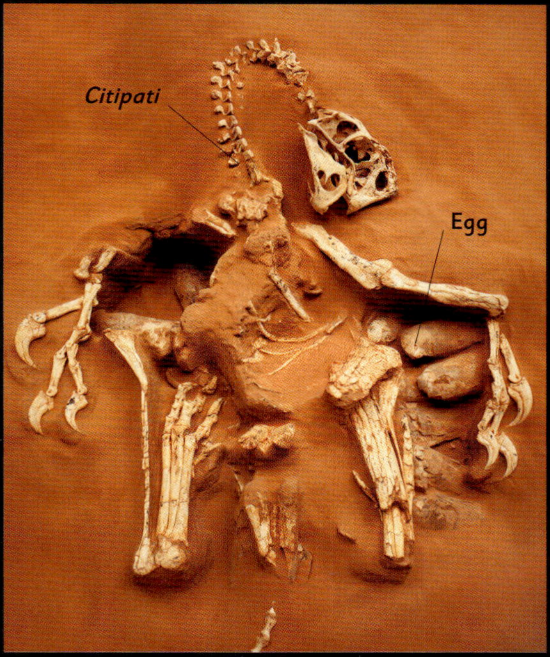

Turn and learn

Parental care of young dinosaurs: **pp. 24–25**

Bringing it back to life

This model recreates the fossilized scene above, showing the *Citipati* shielding her eggs. These dinosaurs had odd-looking beaked snouts. They may have raided other nests for food for themselves and their young.

No. They had hard, brittle shells, like the eggs of birds.

Birth and care of young

We know that some dinosaurs lived in colonies, thanks to finds of fossilized mud nests in Montana, USA. These belonged to *Maiasaura*. The name means "good mother lizard".

Maiasaura

What a discovery!

Jack Horner was one of the palaeontologists who discovered the nests in Montana. He's shown here with a fossilized nest.

Turn and learn
Dinosaurs that lived in groups:
pp. 30-31

Let's look at the nests

The round nests were as wide as a car, 1 m (3 ft) high, and could hold 25 eggs. *Maiasaura* made their nests carefully, each creature forming a large mound with a hollow in it.

It's believed the nests were lined with vegetation.

What sort of dinosaur was *Maiasaura*?

Model of *Maiasaura* nest

Some hatchling fossils had worn teeth, suggesting they had been fed in the nest or had foraged and returned.

It's safer in the nest!

The nests contained trampled eggshells and some had bones of hatchlings, which suggests the young had remained in the nest after hatching. Similarly, many of today's birds remain in their nest until they can look after themselves.

I'm gonna grow!

The hatched babies weighed about as much as a big, heavy book, and were about 30 cm (1 ft) long. The adult dinosaurs weighed as much as a small car and were as long as a bus.

We're hungry!

Experts don't think there were many plants around the nests, so the mothers probably found food elsewhere and brought it back to their young.

Colony life

The nests in Montana were spaced out, suggesting they were part of a colony. The spaces acted as pathways between nests, and allowed the adults to lie next to the eggs to protect them.

It was a hadrosaur. Learn more about them on pages 70–71.

Hunting

Meat-eaters had to scavenge or hunt to stay alive. Some would have hunted alone, but there is also evidence of pack hunting. This does make it easier to corner and overcome prey. Just think how effective lions are at hunting today.

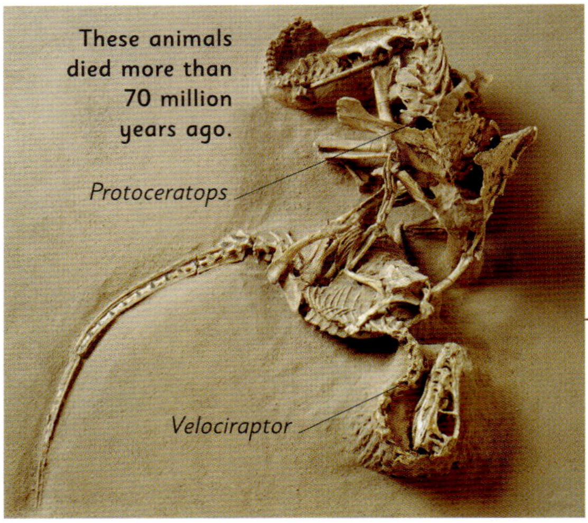

A fight to the death

This amazing fossil captured the death throes of a *Protoceratops* and *Velociraptor* locked in combat. It provides proof that *Velociraptor* preyed on *Protoceratops*.

Fierce hunter

Velociraptor may only have been the size of a large dog, but it was probably an incredibly accomplished killer. Its narrow jaws contained blade-like fangs, and its fingers and toes were armed with dagger-like claws.

Did dinosaurs ever hunt humans?

Let's join up

Scientists believe a number of dinosaurs may have hunted in packs.

Utahraptor was the largest known raptor. It prowled western USA.

Deinonychus was a 3 m (10 ft) long killer that roamed North America.

Giganotosaurus was one of the largest meat-eaters.

Watch out! Rotten teeth!

Some of the large meat-eaters may have delivered a batch of bacteria when they bit. The largest living lizard, the Komodo dragon, has saliva full of bacteria that live on rotting meat stuck in its teeth. Its bite can poison its victim. The same may have applied to some of the dinosaurs.

Komodo dragon

A young *Protoceratops* would have had little chance of defending itself against a hungry *Velociraptor*.

Protoceratops

Go away!

Plant-eating dinosaurs had to find ways to protect themselves against the sharp teeth and claws of meat-eaters. They tended to have tough skin – or armour – and some developed interesting weaponry.

Edmontonia lived in the same places, and at the same time, as *T. rex*, so it needed tough protection!

Walking shields

The armoured dinosaurs, or ankylosaurs, were rather tank-like, with their low-to-ground appearance and heavily plated backs. There was a huge variety.

Chain mail protection

Stegosaurus is instantly recognizable with its bony plates. It also had bony studs under its neck and on its hips, thighs, and tail. These were jointed like chain mail, preventing a meat-eater biting, but allowing the *Stegosaurus* to move.

Stegosaurus

Could the ankylosaurs run away from danger?

Swing that club!

Ankylosaurus had a lump of thickened bone at the end of its tail, giving it a club shape. Its muscular tail would swing this club from side to side. It also had thick bone on its head, neck, and body.

Geysers shoot hot water into the air. They are rare today, but may have been more common in the Mesozoic Era.

Ankylosaurus has been described as a "living tank".

***Ankylosaurus* tail**

Triceratops

Triceratops had a bony shield to protect its neck and shoulders.

Stay back!

Triceratops was one of the largest of all horned dinosaurs. It would have been an intimidating dinosaur to try and kill.

Tail defence

Tails – especially armoured tails – were useful for swinging at predators.

Euoplocephalus had a club made from fused bone at the end of its tail.

Stegosaurus had spikes at the end of its tail that could be 1 m (3 ft) long.

Diplodocus may have used its long tail as a whip.

Scientists don't think they could run fast, so their body armour was their defence.

It's better with friends

Many of today's animals live in groups – some for protection (antelope) and some for hunting (lions). It is likely that many dinosaurs did the same, and for similar reasons.

Herd of *Iguanodon*

It's noisy here

Just imagine the sounds and clouds of dust as large groups of dinosaurs moved off. Herds of cattle can sound like thunder if they stampede. A herd of hefty dinosaurs must have been a jaw-dropping sight.

Large sauropods may have stuck together in big groups.

This way for food!

If dinosaurs did gather together in large groups, it suggests that some may have been migratory – they moved on in search of fresh grazing, much as African wildebeest do today. Large plant-eating sauropods may have trekked massive distances.

How far would dinosaurs have migrated?

Being big and living in a herd help animals protect themselves from attack. Only the weak or young may be picked off.

A dinosaur highway?

In Cretaceous times, an inland sea stretched from north to south through North America. Experts think that the beaches on the western side were used as a migration route, as masses of fossilized dinosaur footprints have been found there.

What's the proof?

Palaeontologists use all sorts of evidence to determine which dinosaurs probably lived in herds.

Lots of bones from the same type of dinosaur are found in the same area.

Fossilized footprints show herds of particular dinosaurs moving together.

Fossilized nesting colonies have been uncovered, notably in Montana, USA.

It is likely that some would migrate long distances of up to 300 km (187 miles).

Triassic dinosaurs

Just before the Triassic period, the Earth suffered a mass extinction (probably caused by climate changes) that wiped out about 96 per cent of all living things. It took millions of years before the planet could even begin to recover.

Triassic Earth as it looked between 252 and 201 million years ago.

Animal life

Mammal-like reptiles of the early Triassic developed into true mammals by the end of the period.

Eozostrodon, one of the earliest true mammals, fed its young with milk.

Lystrosaurus, an early Triassic mammal-like reptile, was a dog-sized plant-eater.

Megazostrodon, a mammal, was about 12 cm (5 in) long. It may have eaten insects.

What did the existence of one huge land mass mean for animal life?

So what was Earth like?

In Triassic times, the planet was hot and dry, with huge deserts. There were pockets of fertile land at the coasts, but there were no flowers. Earth would have been unrecognizable to us.

Herrerasaurus's body shape shows it would have been a fast-moving dinosaur.

Early dinosaurs would have seen huge areas of hot, red desert.

Herrerasaurus is one of the earliest known dinosaurs.

Staurikosaurus

New life appears

The Triassic period saw the gradual renewal of life on Earth, and the appearance of the largest creatures ever to roam there – the dinosaurs.

Picture detective

Look through the Triassic Dinosaurs pages to identify the picture clues below.

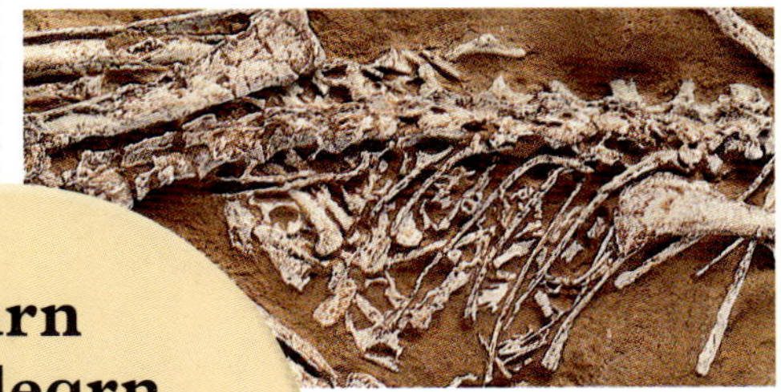

Turn and learn

Eoraptor: **pp. 42–43**

Early mammals: **pp. 96–97**

It meant that land animals were free to roam where they wanted.

The dinosaurs are coming

There were no dinosaurs at the start of the Triassic period. In fact, there was very little life. So where did they come from?

The name "archosaur" means "ruling lizard".

Postosuchus grew to 4.5 m (15 ft) long.

At the start

The dinosaurs were part of a group of reptiles called the archosaurs. One of the largest Triassic archosaurs was the formidable predator, *Postosuchus*.

Saltwater crocodile

An ancient history

Today's crocodiles are the biggest surviving archosaurs. Crocodiles have a similar body shape to the Triassic *Desmatosuchus*. Birds are also archosaurs.

Long shoulder spikes protected the animal's neck.

Desmatosuchus

Early pterosaurs were not much larger than a modern crow.

We were there!

Pterosaurs were flying reptiles, not dinosaurs, and they appeared in late Triassic skies. One of the first pterosaurs was *Peteinosaurus*.

Other archosaurs

Postosuchus was not the only archosaur, though it was the most fearsome.

Lagosuchus was just 30 cm (1 ft) in length.

Euparkeria was slightly larger, at 61 cm (2 ft) in length.

Chasmatosaurus reached lengths of 2 m (6.5 ft).

We are dinosaurs!

Some of the most primitive dinosaurs belong to a group called the coelurosaurs, a name that means "hollow-tailed reptile".

Coelophysis were just 2–3 m (6–10 ft) in length.

Bony plates covered *Desmatosuchus*'s back and tail, and part of its belly.

Weird or what?

Although the mighty *T. rex* did not appear for another 160 million years, it was descended from the coelurosaurs.

No, but it was closely related.

Petrified Forest

The Petrified Forest in Arizona, North America, is packed with late Triassic fossils of plants and animals.

Placerias

Not a dinosaur

The fossils in Arizona give us some idea of the sorts of animals that the first dinosaurs would have met. *Placerias* was a large reptile, growing up to 2.7 m (9 ft) long.

The trees were huge, originally standing at about 60 m (200 ft) in height.

Floodwaters covered the bases of the trees, uprooting many.

Is that a crocodile?

Phytosaurs were crocodile-like reptiles. Some species grew as long as buses – up to 12 m (40 ft).

What dinosaur fossils have been found in the Petrified Forest?

Remains of a forest

Ancient fossilized trees dot the ground in the Petrified Forest. They are all that remain of a once mighty Triassic forest of conifer trees. So how have the trees been preserved for 220 million years?

Chindesaurus had particularly long hind legs.

Over millions of years, the trees were buried in gravelly sand. Gradually, they turned to stone.

Millions of years later the land eroded, exposing the fossilized trunks.

An early dinosaur

Chindesaurus is one of North America's earliest known dinosaurs. It could probably move fast when hunting.

Those of some of the world's first dinosaurs, such as *Chindesaurus* and *Coelophysis*.

Triassic plant-eaters

The Triassic saw the emergence of the prosauropods, an early type of sauropod (a dinosaur group that appeared later).

A long-named prosauropod

Thecodontosaurus was the first Triassic prosauropod to be named. It was a primitive plant-eating dinosaur with saw-edged teeth.

The first large dinosaur

Plateosaurus is believed to have been the first large dinosaur, reaching about 8 m (26 ft) in length. Scientists also think that it was one of the most common of the late Triassic dinosaurs.

Like most prosauropods, *Plateosaurus* was a plant-eater.

Turn and learn
Sauropods: **pp. 50–55**

Where have *Plateosaurus* fossils been found?

I can reach it!

Scientists think that *Plateosaurus* could stand on its back limbs to reach tree leaves. Fossils have been found in groups, suggesting it lived in herds.

Plateosaurus

The word "prosauropod" means "before sauropods".

Ginkgo leaves

Teeth matter

Plateosaurus had small, leaf-shaped teeth set into its jaw. These helped it to shred tough leaves and stems.

Fossil of a *Mussaurus* hatchling

It's just a baby

Mussaurus, whose name means "mouse lizard", hatched from a tiny egg that was 2.5 cm (1 in) long, but grew to 3 m (10 ft) long.

France, Germany, and Switzerland.

From small beginnings

Early plant-eaters were small, but by the end of the Triassic, some grew to huge proportions.

Melanorosaurus, or "black mountain lizard", was a bulky, four-footed plant-eater and possibly one of the first sauropods.

Don't get in the way!

Riojasaurus was a heavily built herbivore that grew to about 9–11 m (30–36 ft) in length. It had a long neck, body, and tail.

Dog-sized

Pisanosaurus was small, and the earliest known ornithishcian dinosaur. It probably fed on low-growing plants.

Could *Riojasaurus* run?

When fully grown, a *Mussaurus* would have weighed some 120 kg (260 lb).

It's so tiny!

Remember *Mussaurus*, which we met on page 39? Here you can see how this baby dinosaur's skull could fit on a fingertip. *Mussaurus* is the smallest fossilized dinosaur skeleton known. Large dinosaurs often started off small, but they grew and grew and grew.

Turn and learn
What Triassic dinosaurs would have seen and eaten: **pp. 10–11**

Riojasaurus had spoon-shaped, serrated teeth.

Teeth talk

Riojasaurus would have used its teeth to pull needles and twigs from conifer trees. It may have swallowed them whole to be ground up in its stomach.

Plodding along

Riojasaurus moved slowly on thick, elephant-like legs. It probably lived in large herds for protection from predators.

Lesothosaurus

This small dinosaur appeared as the Triassic slipped into the Jurassic, making it one of the last Triassic dinosaurs. It lived on into the Jurassic.

Lesothosaurus

Yes, but it would have been unable to run very fast.

We're looking for meat!

As with today's animals, there were more plant-eaters than meat-eaters in the world of the dinosaurs. One of the earliest meat-eaters was the *Eoraptor*.

Old dinosaur bones

Just 1 m (3 ft) long, the fierce *Eoraptor* was only recently discovered and named when a near-complete skeleton was found in Argentina, South America, in 1991. The skeleton had been well-preserved.

What does the name *Eoraptor* mean?

Staurikosaurus

This small meat-eater, or theropod, is another early dinosaur. It was a little bigger than *Eoraptor*, but still slender, and probably only the weight of a 9-year-old child.

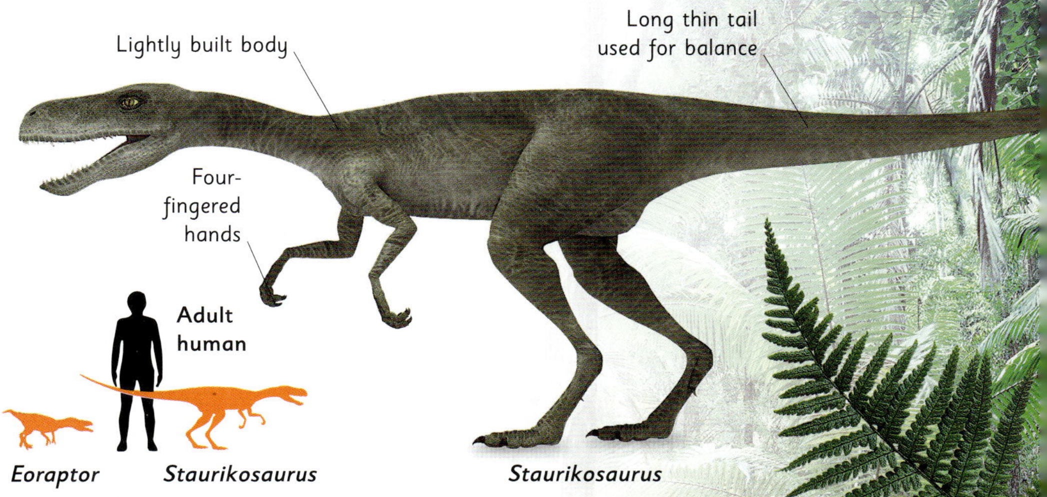

Eoraptor had large eyes, so probably enjoyed good vision.

We're ready to bite

Eoraptor probably ate lizards and small mammal-like reptiles, efficiently tearing into them with its sharp, curved front teeth.

Scientists believe *Eoraptor* lived 228 million years ago.

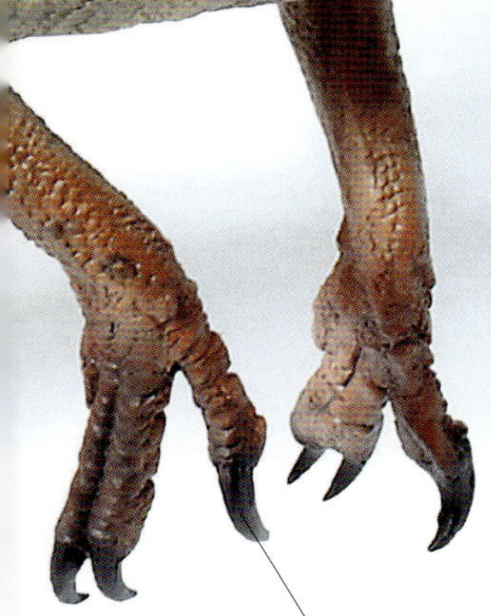

Like many early dinosaurs, *Eoraptor* had five-fingered hands.

Dinosaur claws

As dinosaurs evolved, it seems that the number of fingers on their forelimbs decreased.

Four or five fingers were found on early dinosaurs, such as *Thecodontosaurus*.

Three fingers were found on later dinosaurs, such as *Allosaurus*.

Two fingers were found on many Cretaceous dinosaurs, such as *T. rex*.

Turn and learn
Pack hunters: **pp. 26–27**

"Dawn thief".

Herrera's dinosaur

Find an unknown dinosaur, and it may be named after you. That's what happened to Victorino Herrera after he found fragments of a dinosaur fossil in 1958.

weird or what?

Triassic days were shorter than our days. That's because the Earth spun a little faster in Triassic times. It meant that a Triassic day lasted 22¾ hours rather than 24!

Where did Victorino Herrera find the fragments of *Herrerasaurus*?

What did it eat?

Herrerasaurus probably ate mammal-like reptiles called cynodonts.

Thrinaxodon was a small meat-eater. It may have been hairy.

Cynognathus was a ferocious predator with long, dog-like teeth.

Diademodon was a plant-eater that grew to the size of a small cow.

Pisanosaurus

Looking out for something small

As well as cynodonts, *Herrerasaurus* may have feasted on smaller dinosaurs, such as *Pisanosaurus*. Its light frame would have helped it to be a stealthy hunter.

The jaws were well-designed to grip struggling prey.

Head talk

Herrerasaurus had a long pointed head and sharp, saw-edged teeth. Its jaw was double-hinged to help it grip its prey.

A long tail helped to balance the body.

A rare find

A near-complete skeleton of *Herrerasaurus* was found in 1988 near the Andes mountains, South America. It showed the dinosaur to be one of the largest hunters of its time. It was a little longer than a car.

In Argentina, where he lived.

Ghost Ranch

A fossil quarry in New Mexico is the site of one of the most incredible dinosaur finds ever. Hundreds of dinosaurs died there.

Edwin H Colbert (left) with members of his team.

What was found?

In 1947, Edwin H Colbert documented the discovery of hundreds of well-preserved *Coelophysis* skeletons at Ghost Ranch, New Mexico. This meat-eating dinosaur was one of the Earth's first dinosaurs.

A look at *Coelophysis*

Coelophysis was about 2.4 m (8 ft) long and weighed about 23 kg (50 lb). Its long slender jaws were lined with sharp teeth – evidence that it ate meat.

How did Ghost Ranch get its name?

At Ghost Ranch, *Coelophysis* fossils were discovered under just 60 cm (2 ft) of rock.

Ghost Ranch today

Ghost Ranch is a barren place today, but 220 million years ago it was criss-crossed with rivers prone to flooding.

weird or what?

Some people believe there were hangings at Ghost Ranch, and its desert lands are haunted by the dead.

Fossilized *Coelophysis* skeletons

Groups of skeletons were found together.

Locked in death

The fossilized skeletons were twisted around each other and palaeontologists believe that they all died together, their deaths caused by flash floods.

Large eye sockets suggest *Coelophysis* had keen eyesight.

Were they cannibals?

One *Coelophysis* fossil has a young *Coelophysis* skeleton among its ribs, and it was once thought that adults preyed on younger and weaker members of their own kind. However, this now seems unlikely.

Coelophysis probably walked on its hind limbs and used its forelimbs to catch and hold prey.

The young skeleton can be seen in the animal's stomach area.

The fossil quarry is named after a nearby farm.

Jurassic dinosaurs

During the Jurassic, the supercontinent Pangaea began to break apart. The oceans spread over what had been land, and huge areas flooded. The result was widespread shallow seas and milder weather.

Jurassic Earth as it looked between 201 and 145 million years ago

So what was the Earth like?

Gradually the Earth's habitats became less extreme, encouraging more plant variety and the gradual growth of rainforests. There were fewer areas of desert. Dinosaurs moved to new lands, some roaming huge distances.

Did *T. rex* live during the Jurassic period?

Animal life

The Jurassic saw the appearance of giant plant-eating sauropods, such as *Brachiosaurus, Apatosaurus,* and *Diplodocus*. Large meat-eaters also emerged, with killers such as *Allosaurus* and *Dilophosaurus* ready to eat anything they could catch. The dinosaurs ruled the Earth.

Picture detective

Look through the Jurassic Dinosaurs pages to identify each of the picture clues below.

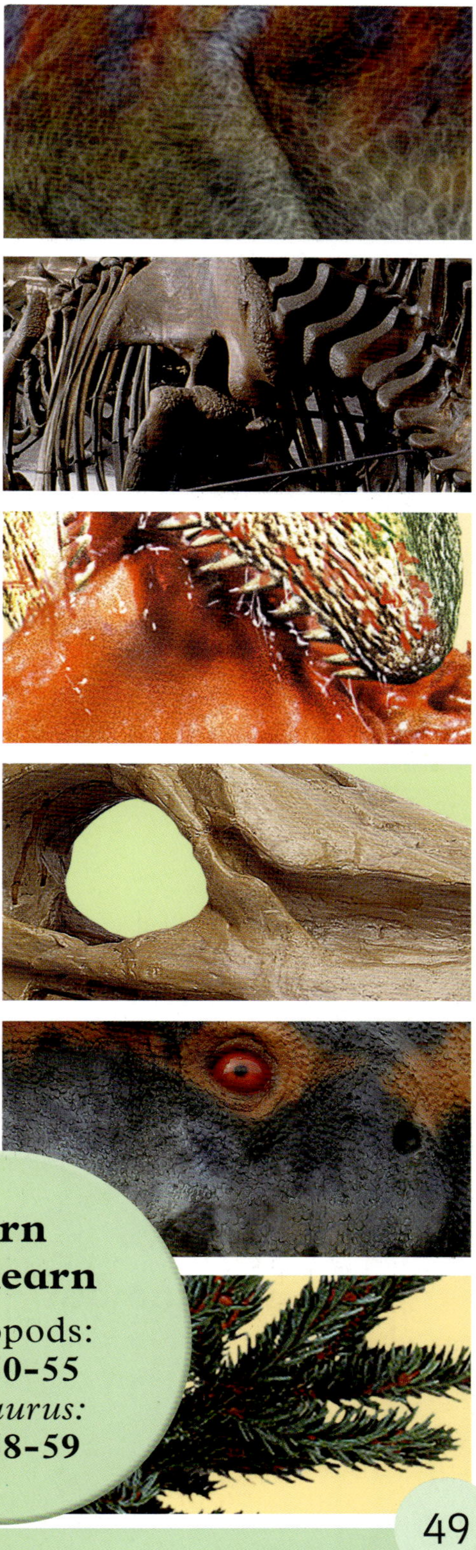

Turn and learn

Sauropods: **pp. 50–55**
Allosaurus: **pp. 58–59**

No, it came later, during the Cretaceous period.

Sauropods

Sauropods were the heaviest, longest, and tallest animals ever to walk on land. They were herbivores, and would have had to graze continually.

Around the world

Sauropods have been found all over the world.

Mamenchisaurus grew to 22 m (72 ft) in length in Jurassic China.

Camarasaurus reached a monstrous 23 m (75 ft) in Jurassic North America.

Barapasaurus grew to lengths of 18 m (59 ft) and roamed Jurassic India.

Vulcanodon was just 6.5 m (21 ft) when it prowled Jurassic Zimbabwe.

Tiny-brained eating machines

Sauropods had tiny heads compared to their bodies. Peg-shaped teeth were used to gather vegetation.

Diplodocus skull

Diplodocus's neck and tail made up most of its length.

Look at the size of it!

Imagine a dinosaur that was as long as a tennis court – an adult *Diplodocus* was!

Diplodocus skeleton

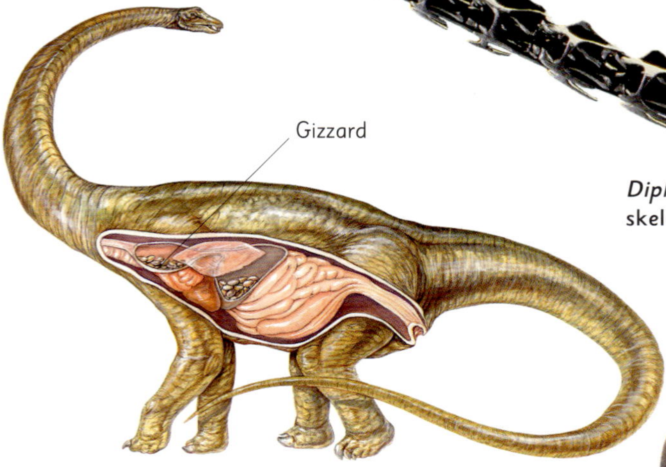

Gizzard stones

Stones in the gut

Like other sauropods, *Diplodocus* may have swallowed stones to help break down tough plant fibres.

How many neck vertebrae did the *Diplodocus* have?

It's like a giraffe!

Brachiosaurus had longer forelimbs than hind limbs, so its back sloped down to its hindquarters – rather like a giraffe. But *Brachiosaurus* could reach two or three times higher than a giraffe.

Up high

Brachiosaurus nibbled leaves at the tops of trees. Its long neck may have helped the *Brachiosaurus* to feed where other plant-eaters could not reach.

Sauropods under attack

A sauropod's size was its defence – a fully grown, healthy adult would have been too large to attack. Some were massive. However, the young and sick were vulnerable.

The height of defence

A *Barosaurus* may have reared up to protect its young. Standing on its hind legs, it would have been as tall as a four-storey building – about 15 m (49 ft).

Replica neck bones of a *Barosaurus* are carried to an exhibition in New York, USA.

Barosaurus

How long could a sauropod live?

A whip in the tail
A tail can make a good whip, and scientists believe that *Apatosaurus* (originally called *Brontosaurus*) may have whipped its tail at predators. This could have resulted in a nasty injury.

A *Diplodocus* was about 33 m (108 ft) long.

Diplodocus used its peg-shaped teeth to strip leaves from tall conifer trees.

On the attack
There was no shortage of Jurassic meat-eating dinosaurs.

Ceratosaurus lived on tree-covered plains and ate dinosaurs and reptiles.

Saurophaganax is thought by scientists to be a type of *Allosaurus*.

Torvosaurus had a bulky body and was the largest carnivore of its time.

Look up!
Diplodocus is the longest dinosaur ever found. It weighed as much as six elephants.

Weird or what?

Diplodocus eggs have been found in lines – not in nests. Scientists believe the animals may have laid their eggs while they walked along!

Allosaurus

Allosaurus bit into its prey, then pulled its head up, tearing away flesh.

Probably about 80 years.

Cetiosaurus

Meet an ancient giant – the *Cetiosaurus.* On a diet of ferns and trees, it grew to huge proportions. Its thigh bone alone was more than 1.8 m (6 ft) – the length of a fully grown man!

We are family!

Like all dinosaurs, *Cetiosaurus* belongs to a family. It is a part of the cetiosauridae family, whose members lived all over the world. Here's one of its Chinese cousins, *Shunosaurus.*

It's not a whale!

Cetiosaurus was the first sauropod to be found and one of the first dinosaurs to be named. Originally, it was believed to be related to the whale because its backbones, or vertebrae, were similar to those of a whale.

Cetiosaurus vertebra

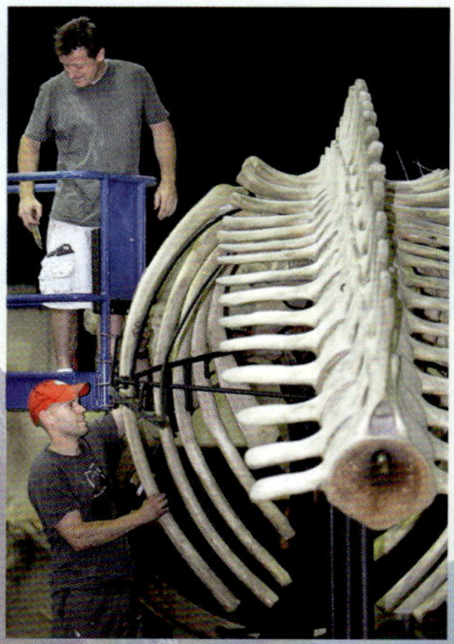

Whale vertebrae

So just how big?

Although only medium-sized for a sauropod, *Cetiosaurus* was an impressive 16 m (53 ft) long. Large herds lived by an ancient sea in the area we now call England.

What does the name *Cetiosaurus* mean?

What about elsewhere?

The huge *Rhoetosaurus* was one of Australia's largest Jurassic dinosaurs. Its great weight meant it probably walked slowly and did not run.

Large feet spread *Rhoetosaurus*'s weight over a wide area.

Hungry predators

A number of hungry Jurassic meat-eaters might have killed and eaten *Cetiosaurus*.

Megalosaurus was 8 m (26 ft) long. It had curved teeth and long, sharp claws.

Eustreptospondylus was 5–6.5 m (16–22 ft) tall. It was a lightly built hunter.

Poekilopleuron was 9 m (30 ft) long with knife-like teeth that sliced into its prey.

Turn and learn
Living in herds:
pp. 30-31

We ate plants, too!

The bulky sauropods weren't the only herbivorous dinosaurs in the Jurassic world. A variety of small, plant-eating dinosaurs were also competing for food.

Other herbivores

Here are some more Jurassic plant-eaters that you may not know.

Heterodontosaurus, the "different-toothed lizard", had three kinds of teeth.

Lufengosaurus had a horse-sized body. It was a sturdily built prosauropod.

Lesothosaurus had a slim body that was only the size of a small goat.

Tough stalks? No problem!

Unlike the sauropods, many smaller plant-eaters had horny, toothless beaks and ridged cheek teeth. They used these to strip tough leaves from woody stems.

Were two legs best?

These small plant-eaters had the ability to walk on two legs. This made them far more agile than the bulky sauropods.

How do we know so much about the plants the dinosaurs ate?

Camptosaurus skeleton

Camptosaurus

I'm a survivor

This dinosaur spans two periods – it survived from the late Triassic into the early Cretaceous in North America and England.

Scutellosaurus

The bony spikes would have made *Scutellosaurus* a lot heavier than other similar-sized dinosaurs.

Don't eat me!

Aside from good agility, some plant-eaters had extra protection. *Scutellosaurus* was covered with more than 300 little bony spikes on its back, sides, and tail.

Dryosaurus

Dryosaurus was perfectly built to run away from danger – fast!

Parrot face

Dryosaurus had a parrot-like beak, which it used to crop plants that it then crushed up with its leaf-shaped teeth. It probably lived in herds in Eastern Africa and North America.

Cycads resembled palms we see today, but they didn't produce flowers.

Conifer trees were plentiful long before the dinosaurs came along.

Horsetails grew taller than many trees in the Mesozoic Era.

Ferns were around long before the appearance of the dinosaurs.

Turn and learn

What dinosaurs saw: **pp. 10-11**

***Lesothosaurus:* p. 41**

We know because there are lots of fossilized plants.

Killers on the loose

Huge and powerful meat-eaters roamed during the Jurassic. Scientists aren't sure if they hunted singly or in packs, but they would have been formidable predators even when hunting alone.

Turn and learn
Triassic meat-eaters: **pp. 42-45**
Cretaceous meat-eater: **pp. 76-77**

Allosaurus
This meat-eater used its good hearing and sense of smell to find a victim. It may have hidden in bushes and jumped out on prey that walked by.

Where was the first almost-complete *Allosaurus* found?

What an odd head!

Dilophosaurus, a large two-legged predator, had a semi-circular bony crest on either side of its skull. These may have helped cool the dinosaur or been used as part of a mating display.

Dilophosaurus prowled long before *Allosaurus* came on the scene.

What a big head!

Allosaurus's head was 1 m (3 ft) long. Special joints allowed the animal to open its jaws extra wide, exposing about 70 teeth, some 10 cm (4 in) long.

A savage hand

Allosaurus's muscled forearms ended in three-digit, grasping hands. They were equipped with savage, hooked claws.

Allosaurus hand fossil

Colorado, USA.

China's killers

Yangchuanosaurus is hunting. This large meat-eater has spotted a weak *Mamenchisaurus,* a supersized plant-eater, and is waiting for its chance to attack.

What's that dinosaur?

Yangchuanosaurus was a large meat-eater that hunted in Jurassic China. With a head the size of an armchair, it would have been a frightening sight.

Deadly dinosaurs

During the Jurassic, dinosaur numbers continued to grow. Here are more meat-eaters from China.

Dilophosaurus, from the early Jurassic, was found in China and the USA.

Monolophosaurus, one of the first giant meat-eaters, was from the mid-Jurassic.

Szechuanosaurus, from the late Jurassic, looked like a small *Allosaurus*.

There's the end

Mamenchisaurus's long neck was supported by 19 vertebrae. That's the highest number of neck bones of any known dinosaur. The bones were hollow; otherwise the neck would have been too heavy to lift.

Famed for its neck

Mamenchisaurus had an absurdly long neck. In fact, its neck was more than half the length of the whole animal and it is currently known as the longest-necked animal ever. Its head, in comparison, was tiny.

weird or what?

The Moon was a little closer to the Earth in Triassic and Jurassic times, making it appear larger in the sky. It would have reflected more of the Sun's light, and so have appeared brighter.

Plants including conifers, seed ferns, club mosses, and horsetails.

Little and large

Although they would not have met, *Compsognathus* and *Ceratosaurus* both lived during the Jurassic – one on warm islands and one on floodplains.

Fossilized *Compsognathus*

Fossil evidence

Compsognathus was found in 1861, but not at first recognized as a dinosaur as it was thought to be too small. One fossil was found with its last meal inside it – a lizard.

Living quarters

Compsognathus lived on a group of islands that were where Europe is now. It was a fierce (though small) predator.

Ceratosaurs

Ceratosaurus belongs to a family of dinosaurs called ceratosaurs. Other members may include:

Dilophosaurus was almost 6 m (20 ft) long and weighed as much as a horse.

Segisaurus was a small ceratosaur, at just 1 m (3 ft) long.

Coelophysis was about 1.8 m (6 ft) long and looked like a long-legged bird.

Ceratosaurus

Ceratosaurus was 4.5–6 m (15–20 ft) long. It was a powerful meat-eating dinosaur with a short horn on its head.

Ceratosaurus means "horned lizard".

Turn and learn
Fossils:
pp. 100-101

A national monument

From 1909 to 1924, scientists removed 300 tonnes (295 tons) of late Jurassic dinosaur bones from a quarry in Utah, USA. The importance of the find was recognized by the creation of the Dinosaur National Monument there in 1915.

Bones in the wall

The Dinosaur National Monument has a visitor's centre built around a wall that contains more than 1,500 dinosaur fossils.

A different landscape

In dinosaur times, the area where the fossils were found was a watering hole. That's why so many creatures gathered there.

How long do you think it took Earl Douglass to remove the *Apatosaurus* skeleton he found?

Apatosaurus lived about 150 million years ago.

Apatosaurus

Apatosaurus had a thick, muscular neck.

The bony plates would have made this dinosaur appear much bigger than it actually was.

Stegosaurus

Broad hind foot with three short toes.

Plant-eaters

Three-quarters of the bones found at the monument belong to sauropods, such as *Apatosaurus*, *Camarasaurus*, and *Diplodocus*.

Earl the explorer

We know about the Utah quarry thanks to a man called Earl Douglass, who was hunting for dinosaur fossils in the area in 1909. His first discovery was an *Apatosaurus*. That was just the beginning!

Meat-eaters

Three types of meat-eaters were found at the Dinosaur National Monument.

Ceratosaurus had a bony horn on its nose. It was a big dinosaur.

Ornitholestes probably preyed on small lizards.

Allosaurus was a large meat-eater. Learn more on page 59.

I recognize that one!

A complete *Stegosaurus* skeleton was found at the monument. This was a small-headed plant-eater that has become famous for its bony plates.

It took him six years.

Cretaceous dinosaurs

Cretaceous Earth as it looked between 145 and 66 million years ago.

At this time, the Earth's continents had separated and were beginning to drift apart. On each one, dinosaurs developed in different ways, so the number of different types of dinosaurs increased significantly.

So what was Earth like?

The beginning of the Cretaceous period saw similar temperatures to those in the Jurassic, but over the next million years or so, temperatures began to cool. The Earth we know was beginning to emerge.

What is the oldest flowering plant found so far called and where was its fossil found?

Animal life

The Cretaceous period saw a huge variety of dinosaurs, from plant-eaters such as *Corythosaurus* and *Triceratops* to meat-eaters such as *Troodon* and *T. rex*. They were the last big dinosaurs to live on Earth, and they flourished.

Picture detective

Look through the Cretaceous Dinosaurs pages to identify each of the picture clues below.

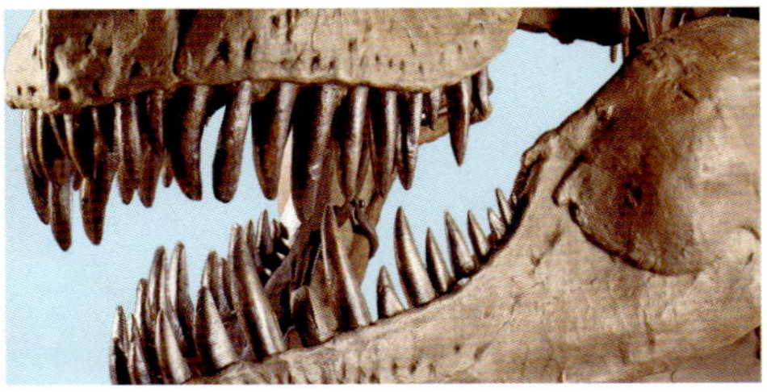

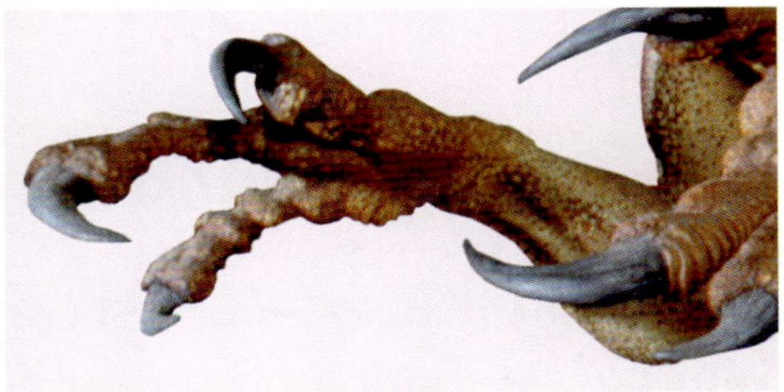

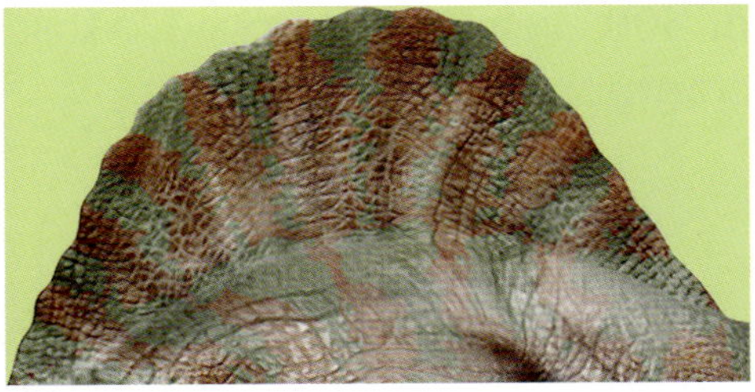

Turn and learn

Troodon: **pp. 82–83**
Horned dinosaurs: **pp. 72–73**

It is called *Archaefructus sinensis*. Its 125-million-year-old-fossil was found in China.

Dinosaur Provincial Park

Today, Dinosaur Provincial Park in Alberta, Canada, is rocky and fairly bare. Seventy-five million years ago, it was a sub-tropical paradise, based around the marshy mouth of a river. It was also the site of an incredible amount of dinosaur activity.

Dinosaur Provincial Park has proved a treasure trove for dinosaur fossils since the first find in 1910.

Fossilized *Corythosaurus* skeleton

Fabulous fossilization

Many of the Park's dinosaur skeletons have been well-preserved because of the original marshy ground – just look at this *Corythosaurus,* a hadrosaur.

What's been found?

Thirty-five species of late Cretaceous dinosaurs have been found at the Park, and a total of 300 skeletons removed. Most common were hadrosaurs.

It's a tank!

Euoplocephalus, a plant-eater, was well protected from a possible attack.

Turtle fossil

What else was found?

In addition to dinosaurs, scientists have found the fossilized skeletons of many other Cretaceous creatures at the Park. These include lots of fish, crocodiles, pterosaurs, birds, mammals, and turtles.

He'll eat me!

Albertosaurus was the Park's largest predator. It would have had plenty of hadrosaurs to feed on.

Albertosaurus looked a little like *T. rex*. In fact, it was related to *T. rex* but it appeared first.

Armoured tanks

Three kinds of ankylosaur dinosaurs have been found at Provincial Park.

Panoplosaurus had long shoulder spikes, as well as bony plates on its back.

Edmontonia was covered with rows of bony plates and spikes.

Euoplocephalus used a hefty lump of bone on its tail for protection.

Broad diet

Pachycephalosaurus (see p. 20) had different types of teeth, which may mean that it ate different types of food, such as plants, nuts and fruit.

More than 170 different types of plants grew in the area.

Pachycephalosaurus

Turn and learn

Ankylosaurs: **pp. 74–75**
Hadrosaurs: **pp. 70–71**

Most ankylosaurs were heavily armoured.

Cretaceous cows

Hadrosaurs, which grazed on all fours, were basically the cows of the Cretaceous. They would have been a familiar sight in North America.

All sorts of crests

Those striking crests came in all sorts of different shapes.

Corythosaurus had a plate-like crest.

***Tsintaosaurus*'s** crest may have been covered in brightly coloured skin.

Lambeosaurus had a helmet-like crest.

Hadrosaurs had stiff tails. It is unlikely these were swung from side to side.

Male hadrosaurs probably had larger crests than the females.

Parasaurolophus

What a sight!

Hadrosaurs are known for having some of the strangest heads of all dinosaurs; many of them had a crest.

Turn and learn

Another hadrosaur, *Maiasaura*: **pp. 24–25**

Can you think of any crested animals today?

A hadrosaur had more than 1,000 teeth (though not all were in use at the same time).

Did they have teeth?

The beaky jaws contained tightly packed rows of teeth to grind vegetation.

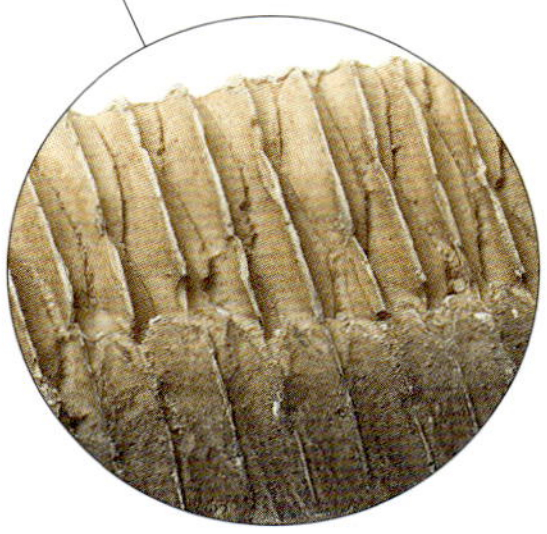

Fossilized hadrosaur teeth

What did they eat?

One hadrosaur fossil contained the remains of its last meal – bark, pine cones, conifer needles, and branches. Such tough plant matter is particularly hard to digest.

Corythosaurus

Chew and move on

A hadrosaur such as *Corythosaurus* would have roamed in huge herds, grazing on leaves, pine needles, and ferns.

A number of lizards and birds have crests.

Horns and frills

Built like a rhinoceros, *Triceratops* is one of the best-known of all dinosaurs. It belongs to a group known as the "horned face" dinosaurs or ceratopsians.

In the big league

Triceratops was one of the largest of all the horned faces, reaching about 10 m (33 ft) in length when fully grown.

What does the name *Triceratops* mean?

Other ceratopsians

There were a number of different dinosaurs with horns and frills.

Protoceratops had a head frill but lacked a horn.

Styracosaurus, or "spiked lizard", had a fancy, horned frill.

Pentaceratops had an enormous neck frill and three long horns.

Sheep of the Gobi

Protoceratops roamed the Gobi Desert in Asia rather as sheep roam today. In fact, they were about the size of sheep.

Like all the horned-face dinosaurs, *Protoceratops* had a parrot-like beak.

That's not a fighter

Protoceratops lacked any protection. Its small size would have made it the ideal prey for a number of meat-eaters.

Fully developed skull

Here you can see the growth of a *Protoceratops* skull, from baby to a fully grown adult.

Hatchling's skull

A big graveyard

The Gobi Desert is littered with the remains of *Protoceratops*, and they show all stages of growth.

"Three-horned face".

Ankylosaurus skull

Armoured tanks

The ankylosaurs were the armoured tanks of the dinosaur world. These four-legged dinosaurs had their own form of protection as they were covered in thick bony plates and spikes.

Armoured head

Ankylosaurs were protected from head to tail. Just look at the solid appearance of these fossilized skulls.

Euoplocephalus skull

Armoured giant

At one time, *Euoplocephalus* was a common ankylosaur on the plains of North America. This creature was well protected from predators as it had fused bony plates over its neck and back.

Euoplocephalus

Were ankylosaurs meat-eaters or plant-eaters?

Ankylosaurs

Ankylosaurs can be separated into groups depending on their appearance. Below are three main groups.

Ankylosaurids, such as *Ankylosaurus*, had bony clubs on their tails.

Nodosaurids, such as *Edmontonia*, had rows of spikes on their bodies.

Polacanthids, such as *Gastonia*, had spiky bodies and tails.

Impressions in rock show that *Saltasaurus* had bony studs.

Saltasaurus

Armoured sauropods, too!

The ankylosaurs were not the only Cretaceous dinosaurs to have armour. Some sauropods did, too. Just look at this studded *Saltasaurus*.

Ankylosaurus tail club

Clubbed tail

Some ankylosaurs had a tail club made of fused bone that they would swing at attackers. The weighty club would have been a formidable weapon.

T. rex

The mighty *T. rex* roamed North America in the last couple of million years that dinosaurs ruled the planet.

T. rex's eyeballs were the size of a clenched fist.

When teeth broke, new ones grew to replace them.

Titanic teeth

T. rex had awesome curved teeth, each as long as a human hand. Altogether, it had 58 of these pointed weapons.

T. rex **preyed on plant-eaters such as *Triceratops*.**

T. rex walked on its powerful hind limbs.

Was it a killer?

We don't really know if *T. rex* was a hunter or a scavenger. It may have attacked and killed, or it may have picked at dead or dying dinosaurs. It may have done both.

T. rex is short for *Tyrannosaurus rex*. What does it mean?

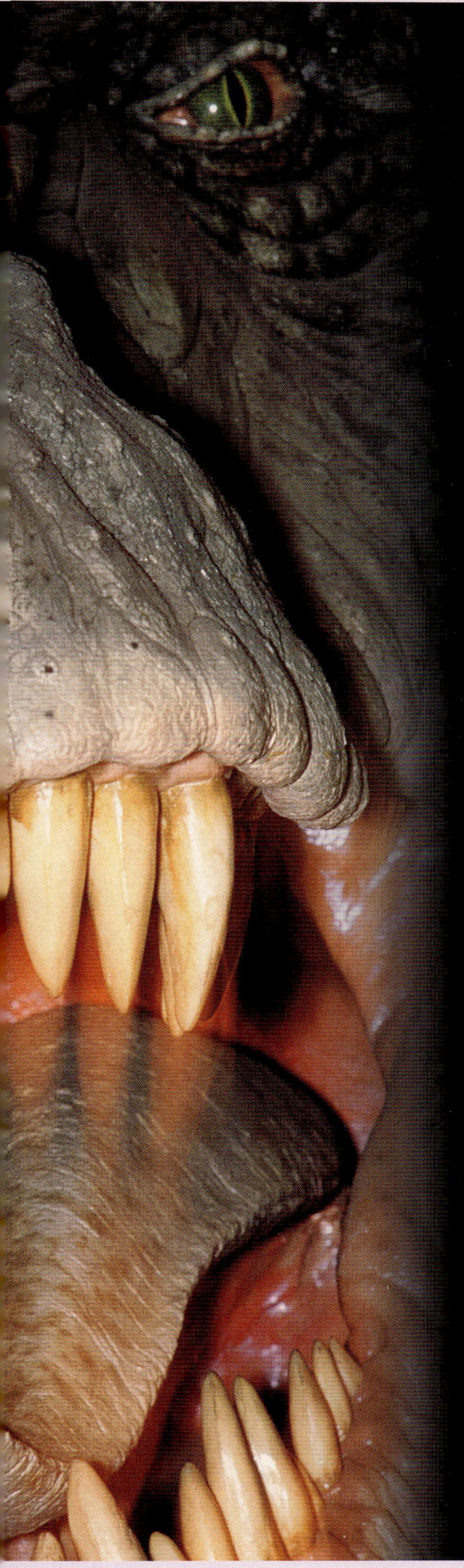

Lighten up

With its massive skull that was 1.5 m (5 ft) long, this beast could swallow small dinosaurs whole! Spaces between the skull bones made it lighter.

A *T. rex* had tiny serrations on its teeth. Its bite would have torn into a victim's flesh.

Guanlong was just 1.1 m (3.6 ft) tall, and most of that was tail and neck!

My ancestor

One of the oldest members of the tyrannosaur family was recently found in China. *Guanlong* prowled Earth some 100 million years before *T. rex*.

What a whopper!

Meet Sue, the world's largest and most complete *T. rex* skeleton. She was sold to an American museum in 1991 for a jaw-dropping £5.3 million ($8 million).

Nose to tail, Sue measures 12.8 m (42 ft).

Tyrannosaurus rex means "king of the tyrant lizards".

Big and bold

Giganotosaurus means "giant southern reptile", and this dinosaur was big. In fact, it may have been larger than *T. rex*. However, the two never met as *Giganotosaurus* was roaming some 10 million years before *T. rex*!

It's a new find!

Giganotosaurus bones were first unearthed in Argentina in the early 1990s, but no complete skeleton has ever been found.

Giganotosaurus would have had a keen sense of smell and excellent eyesight.

weird or what?

It's difficult to imagine just how big and heavy a fully grown *Giganotosaurus* really was. It's thought to have been as heavy as about 125 adult humans. That's a lot of people!

Where did *Giganotosaurus* live?

Did it look like that?

Nobody actually knows what colour any particular dinosaur was. *Spinosaurus* could have been a dull shade, or it may have been more brightly decorated.

Spinosaurus may have been as colourful and patterned as some of the snakes we see today.

Spinosaurus was closely related to *Baryonyx* (see p. 88).

Spinosaurus had crocodile-like teeth, and preyed on fish by wading into the water.

We are family

There was a great variety of size within dinosaur groups. *Spinosaurus,* which was bigger than *T. rex,* belonged to a group of dinosaurs called the spinosaurs. One of *Spinosaurus*'s smallest relatives was a South American dinosaur called *Irritator.*

Fossil remains of *Irritator* have been found in Brazil.

weird or what?

Irritator got its strange name after an irritating episode when its fossilized remains were altered by its finder in an attempt to make it more valuable.

It was found in Egypt, in 1912.

A bright spark?

Troodon is believed to have been the most intelligent of the dinosaurs, given the size of its brain in relation to its body.

Night hunter?

Scientists believe *Troodon* had good vision. It may even have had vertical pupils (just like a cat's) that would have helped it to hunt at night.

Models of *Troodon*

Troodon's long slender limbs would have made it extremely agile.

A large sickle-shaped claw on *Troodon's* second toe was used to tear and slash.

Turn and learn
Dinosaur eggs and nests: **pp. 22–23**

What might *Troodon* have hunted?

Troodon tooth

Let's look at a tooth

"*Troodon*" means "wounding tooth". The small teeth were serrated and hooked backwards to help *Troodon* grip struggling prey.

A *Troodon* had about 120 teeth in its mouth. A human child has 20.

Troodon was probably feathered.

Grab and go

Troodon had three-fingered hands tipped with sharp claws that would have been ideal for grabbing and then holding onto its prey.

My nest!

There is evidence that *Troodon* lived in large colonies, caring for their young. Suspected *Troodon* nests found in Montana, USA, were 1.8 m (6 ft) wide and contained up to 24 eggs.

Probably baby dinosaurs, small mammals, snakes, lizards, and birds.

Meet the raptors

Aggressive and speedy, *Velociraptor* was a formidable predator in late Cretaceous Asia. Although small, it was armed with razor-sharp teeth and terrifying dagger-like claws.

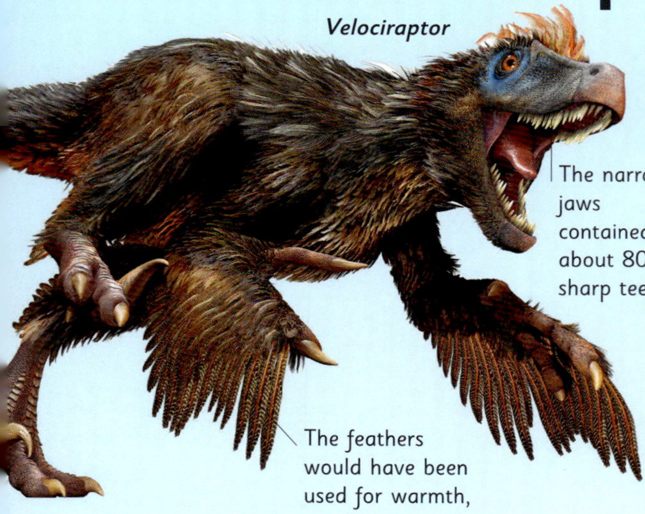

Velociraptor

The narrow jaws contained about 80 sharp teeth.

The feathers would have been used for warmth, not flight.

A feathered dinosaur?

Some dinosaur fossils have been found with traces of a feather-like covering, and it's thought that *Velociraptor* may have had feathers, though no *Velociraptor* fossil has been found with them.

Bambiraptor

Experts believe that *Deinonychus* were one of the more intelligent dinosaurs. They had a lightweight body and long hind legs.

The killer claw

Deinonychus had a vicious killer claw on each of its hind legs. It held the claw off the ground, and slashed its victims with it.

Deinonychus foot fossil

What does the name *Velociraptor* mean?

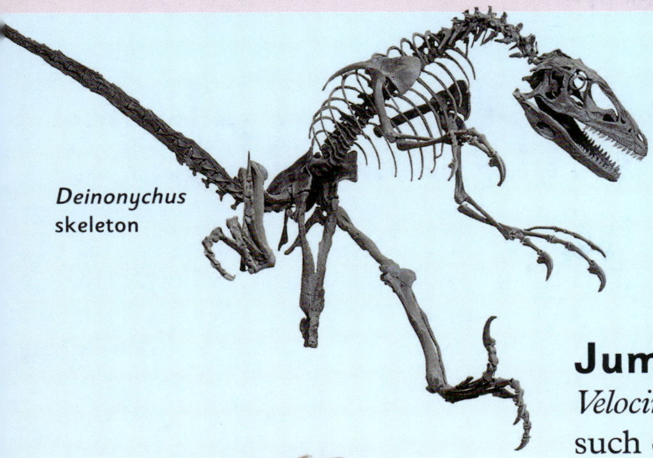

Deinonychus skeleton

This skeleton has been mounted to show *Deinonychus* leaping towards a victim, claws ready.

Jump and grab

Velociraptor and its relations, such as the larger *Deinonychus*, may have hunted in packs and jumped onto the back of their prey, all four limbs extended.

weird or what?

Velociraptor and *Deinonychus* belong to a group called the dromaeosaurids. Scientists believe these killing machines were related to the birds alive today.

Deinonychus means "terrible claw".

"Speedy thief". Scientists believe it may have reached 65 kph (40 mph).

A pot-bellied dinosaur!

Is this the most bizarre of all the dinosaurs? *Therizinosaurus* certainly had the longest known arms, tipped with fingers that had claws up to 60 cm (2 ft) long.

A strange cousin

An odd-looking dinosaur from the same family as *Therizinosaurus* was *Beipiaosaurus*. Evidence shows that its arms and legs were covered with downy feathers.

Leatherback turtle

Are they flippers?

Therizinosaurus had such strange-looking arms that when its claws were first found, they were believed to belong to a giant turtle.

Do you think *Therizinosaurus* was a meat-eater or a plant-eater?

Puzzle time

Scientists have had to piece together an idea of what the *Therizinosaurus* looked like as very little has been found (in fact, only the arms!). Its appearance in books today is based upon finds of other members of the therizinosaur family. Ideas may change.

Recent studies have found that *Therizinosaurus* may have had fine feathers. We don't know for certain.

A plant-eater. It looked threatening, but it had a toothless beak.

Fish for tea

Ninety million years ago, a dinosaur stands watching, silently, by a large lake. Suddenly claws flash in the sunlight, and a fish the length of your leg, a *Lepidotes*, is caught. Meet the fishing dinosaur, *Baryonyx*!

Fishy tale

Lepidotes was a Mesozoic fish that was found in lakes and shallow seas. *Lepidotes* teeth are a common fossil find in Southern England, where they are known as toadstones.

Did it really eat fish?

Baryonyx's crocodile-like jaws were perfect for grabbing fish, but we also know it ate fish because fossilized fish scales and bones were found with this dinosaur's fossil.

How did toadstones get their name?

Look at that claw!

Baryonyx's name means "heavy claw". It was given this name because of its huge thumb claws. The long, curved claws were ideal for stabbing and snatching fish from the water.

Baryonyx's claw measures 30 cm (12 in) along the outside edge.

I found it first

The first fossilized claw of *Baryonyx* was found in England in the early 1980s by an amateur fossil collector called William Walker.

The jaw contains 96 pointed teeth.

Fossilized *Baryonyx* skull

Hidden secrets

After the claw was found, about 60 per cent of the dinosaur was gradually uncovered in surrounding rocks, including this near-perfect skull.

Hundreds of years ago, people thought they came from the heads of living toads!

Other forms of life

When dinosaurs were around, there were other prehistoric creatures also, some of which swam in the sea or flew. So what other creatures co-existed with the dinosaurs?

Life, but not as we know it

Throughout the Mesozoic Era, dinosaurs existed alongside other groups of animals that lived on land and in the oceans, such as mammals and other reptiles. Some of these reptiles could fly.

Would dinosaurs have eaten pterosaurs?

Pterosaurs existed from the late Triassic period to the end of the Cretaceous period.

Plesiosaurs were most common during the Jurassic period.

Picture detective

Look through the Other Forms of Life pages to identify each of the picture clues below.

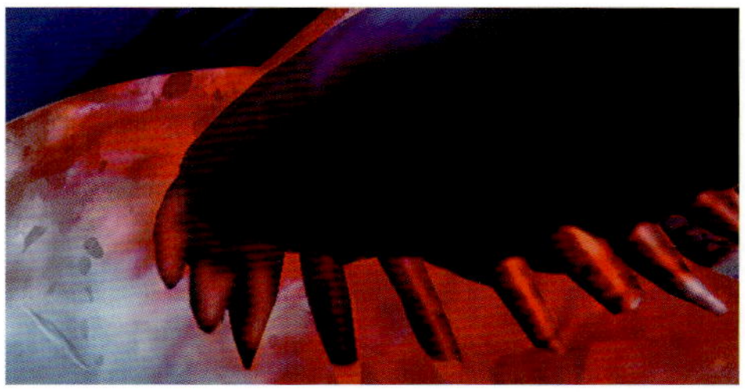

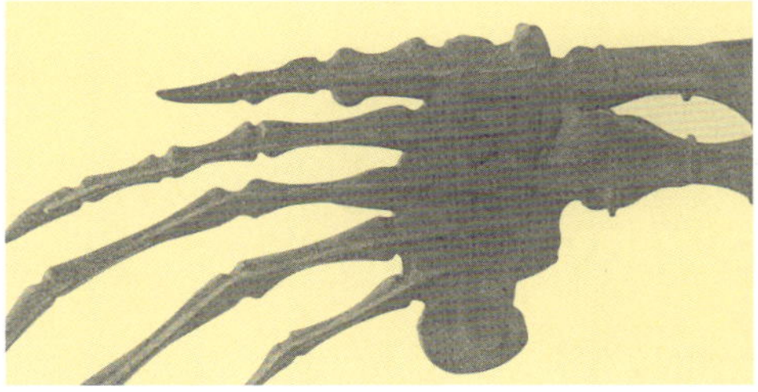

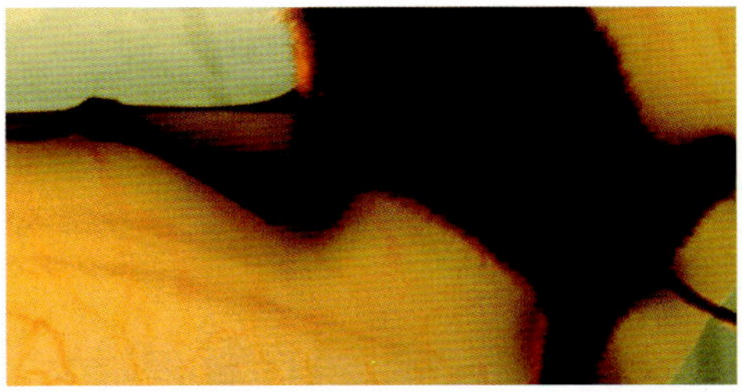

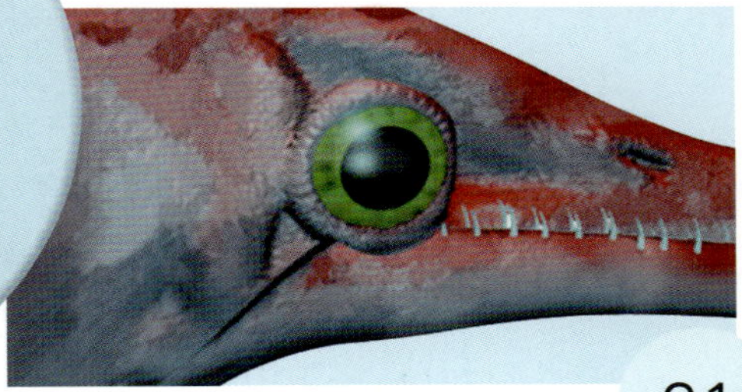

Turn and learn
Plesiosaurs: **pp. 92–93**
Pterosaurs: **pp. 94–95**

Yes, if they managed to catch them!

Monsters of the deep

Ichthyosaurus

There may have been no marine dinosaurs, but an astonishing variety of toothed giant reptiles ruled the seas while the dinosaurs ruled the land.

Elasmosaurus was air-breathing, and just like whales today, it had to come to the surface to breathe.

Its neck was as long as its body.

Ichthyosaurs had large eyes.

Swim away...
An *Ichthyosaurus* used to move swiftly to avoid being eaten. The swimming ichthyosaurs, including *Ichthyosaurus* itself, were perfectly suited for chasing fast-moving prey, such as squid. However, they were vulnerable to attack from larger marine reptiles.

... from danger!
Watch out! A *Liopleurodon* is attacking the ichthyosaurs from below. Perhaps the largest sea-based predator of all time, *Liopleurodon* was a short-necked plesiosaur.

What did *Liopleurodon* eat?

Elasmosaurus

What's that?

Elasmosaurus was also a plesiosaur, but it was long-necked. Its four paddle-shaped limbs propelled it easily through the water. It grew up to 14 m (46 ft) in length.

I recognize that!

Many Mesozoic occupants of the Earth's seas would have been familiar to us.

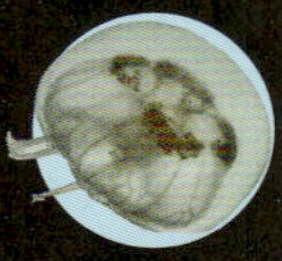

Jellyfish have been around for about 400 million years.

Corals are fragile animals, but they have managed to survive since the dinosaurs.

The **great white shark**'s ancestors date back to the Cretaceous period.

Squid were on the menu for ichthyosaurs, shown by fossil evidence.

Snails are also present in fossil form, showing they too are great survivors.

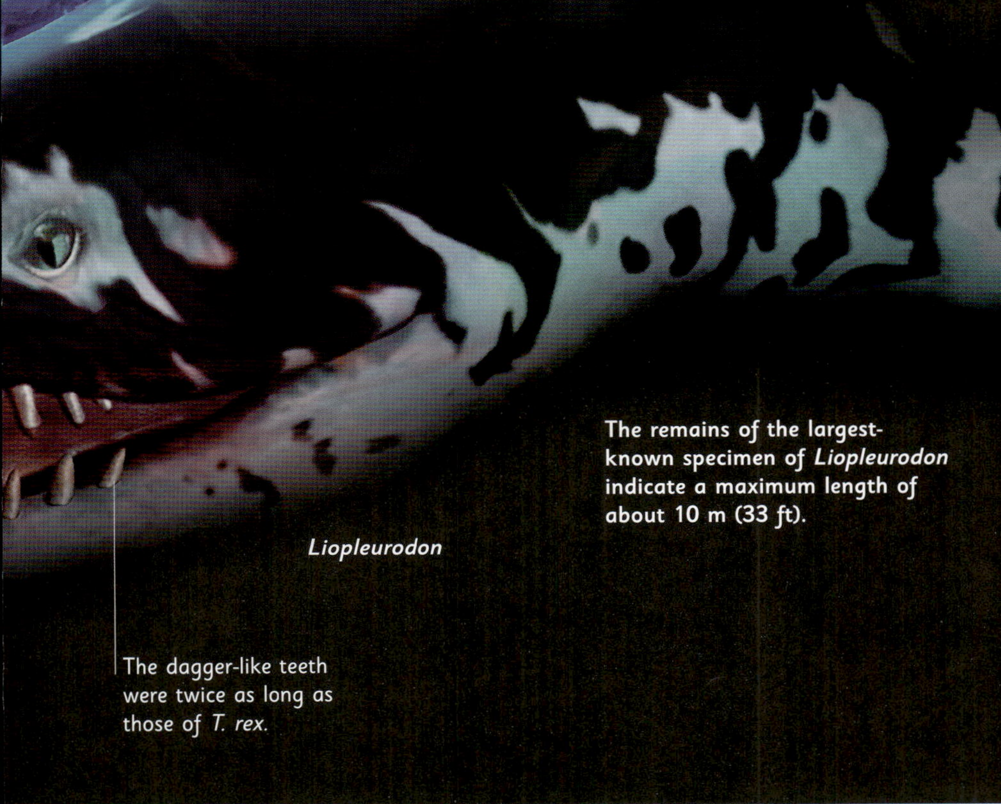

Liopleurodon

The remains of the largest-known specimen of *Liopleurodon* indicate a maximum length of about 10 m (33 ft).

The dagger-like teeth were twice as long as those of *T. rex*.

weird or what?

Some people think the "monster" in Loch Ness, a Scottish Lake, is a plesiosaur that was trapped there when the sea receded millions of years ago!

Anything it could catch, including pterosaurs who flew too close to the water's surface.

Monsters of the air

No dinosaur flew, but they had relatives that did – the pterosaurs, or flying reptiles. Some were tiny, but others had the wingspan of a small aeroplane.

Who came first?

Early pterosaurs had long tails and narrow wings. They were fairly small – *Dimorphodon* and *Rhamphorhynchus* were about 1 m (3 ft) in length.

What did they eat?

Lots of pterosaur fossils have been found in coastal areas, suggesting they swooped low over the sea, picking off fish. They probably also caught insects.

Were pterosaurs a type of bird?

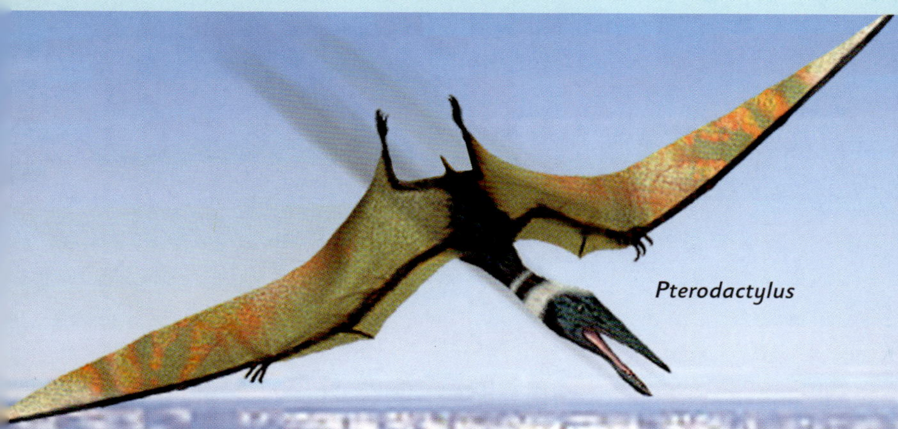
Pterodactylus

Look at mine!

Many Cretaceous pterosaurs had crests. They may have been used to attract mates.

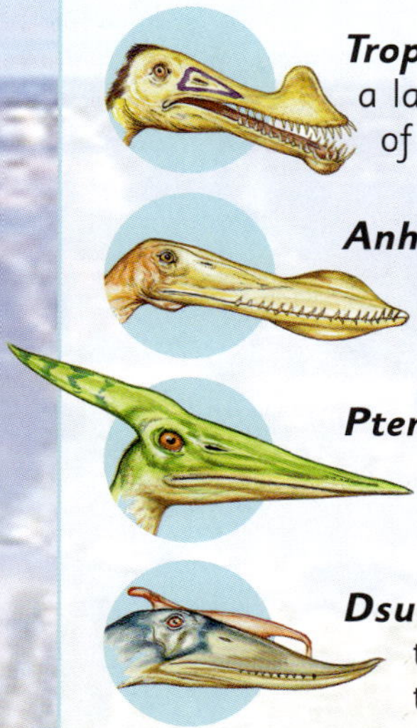

Tropeognathus had a large crest at the end of its upper jaw.

Anhanguera had a crest on its upper and lower jaw.

Pteranodon had a long, backward-pointing crest.

Dsungaripterus had two crests on the top of its head.

Did they have fur?

The pterosaurs probably had fur, like modern-day bats. They also had large eyes, giving them excellent vision.

Tropeognathus

It's the size of a plane!

A male *Tropeognathus* may have had a wingspan of 6 m (20 ft), though it weighed less than a seven-year-old child.

Quetzalcoatlus

Each wing was made of skin that grew between the leg and an extra-long bone of the fourth finger.

Who was the biggest?

By the Cretaceous period, pterosaurs had grown bigger. Possibly the largest flying reptile of all was found in Texas in the 1930s. *Quetzalcoatlus* had a wingspan of 12–14 m (39–46 ft).

No. Pterosaurs were winged reptiles and were not related to birds.

Were there mammals?

Mammals began to appear in the late Cretaceous period, but they were small and were dominated by the success of the dinosaurs. They were to become incredibly successful eventually, but it took millions of years.

Are they really that small?

Primitive mammals began to appear in the late Triassic, some 220 million years ago, and they were tiny. Just look at the mammal timeline shown below with its comparison to the size of an adult human's hand. These mammals were probably nocturnal, hiding in leaf litter and hunting for insects and maybe even dinosaur eggs.

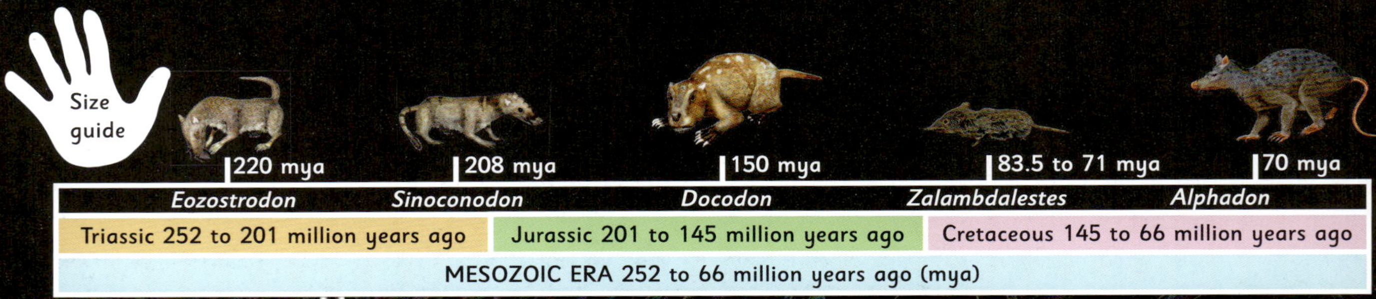

Early mammals probably raided dinosaur eggs if they had the chance.

Why would early mammals have been nocturnal?

When did mammals get big?

The first large predatory mammals, the creodonts, didn't emerge until Palaeocene times (the period of time after the extinction of the dinosaurs).

Did mammals eat dinosaurs?

Palaeontologists recently found a fossilized *Repenomamus*, a badger-sized beast. That's enormous for a Mesozoic mammal! It even had the remains of baby dinosaurs in its gut.

Lookalike

Another early mammal was the platypus-like *Steropodon*. Like the platypus today, this mammal probably laid eggs.

Early mammals, such as *Docodon*, walked on all fours, had long tails, and long bodies and snouts.

weird or what?

Dinosaurs were amazingly successful – they ruled the Earth for 180 million years. Humans emerged some 200,000 years ago. That's a tiny amount of geological time.

This would have allowed them to avoid being eaten by reptiles and dinosaurs.

Size matters

The creatures that lived during the Mesozoic Era varied dramatically in size – some were tiny, but others grew to enormous proportions.

That's not so big...
Ichthyosaurs varied in size. Some were as small as your arm, while many were the size of a dolphin.

Ichthyosaurs are one of the best-known of all Mesozoic creatures.

Mononykus skull

Is that its skull?
Some dinosaurs were really small. This little dinosaur's skull is shown life-size.

... but that's a giant!
However, in Triassic times, ichthyosaurs reached massive proportions.

The largest ichthyosaur was 23 m (75 ft) in length.

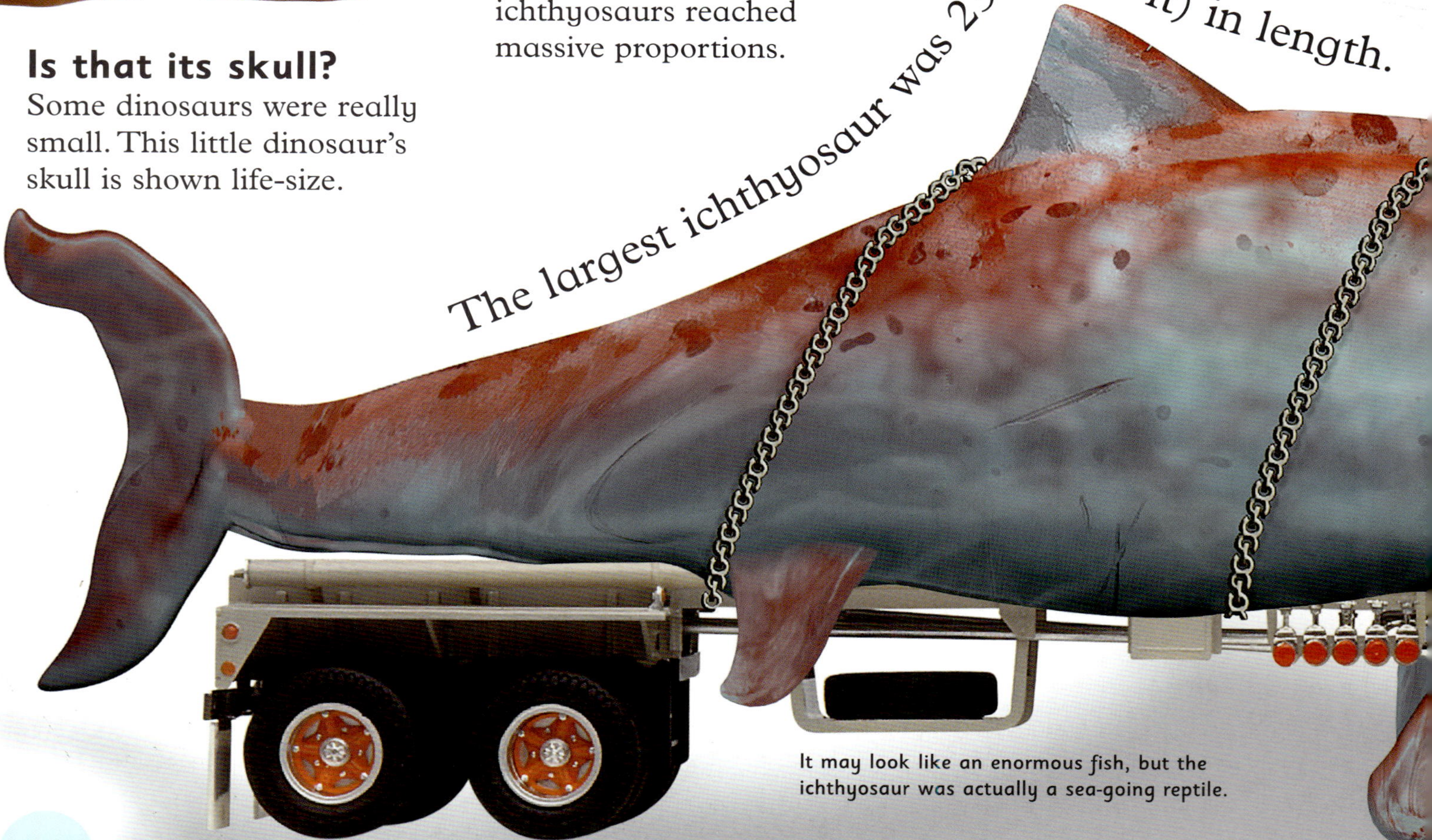

It may look like an enormous fish, but the ichthyosaur was actually a sea-going reptile.

Was the largest ichthyosaur longer than a blue whale?

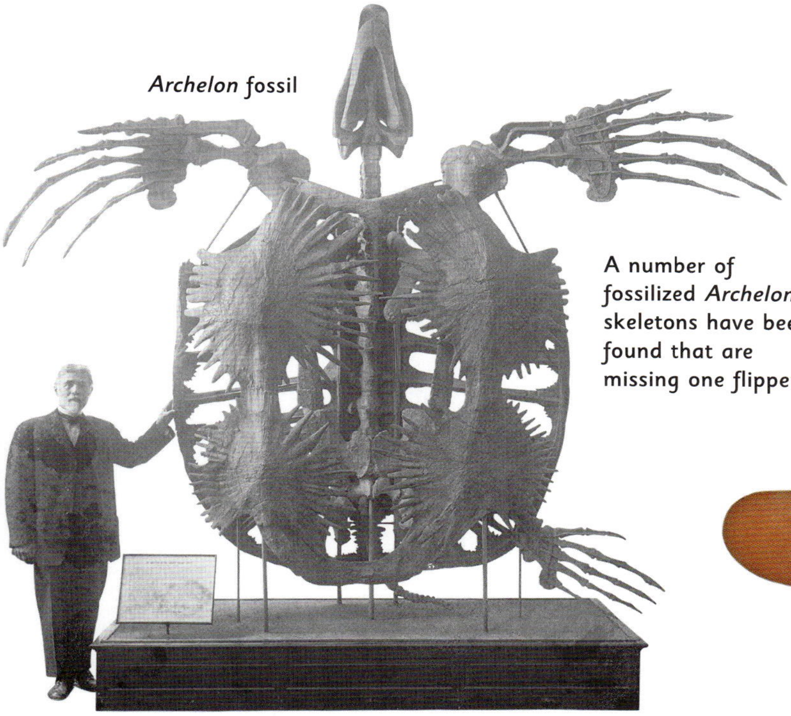

Archelon fossil

A number of fossilized *Archelon* skeletons have been found that are missing one flipper.

Is that a turtle?

Archelon was a turtle, but it was three times the size of the largest turtle today. Fully grown adults had shells that were 4 m (13 ft) long.

It's a tiny opossum

Alphadon was one of the first marsupials (animals that carry their young in pouches). Kangaroos are also marsupials – but *Alphadon* was tiny.

Alphadon

It lived 210 million years ago.

Ichthyosaurs may have had reddish-brown skin.

Turn and learn
Ichthyosaurs: **p. 92**

No. They were big, but blue whales reach 30 m (100 ft) in length.

Fossils

Fossils have been found all over the world, but they are not easy to recognize and have often been discovered by accident, perhaps following building work.

The right conditions?

Lots of fossils have been found, but for every fossilized dinosaur, hundreds and thousands died, decayed, and left no trace.

"Fossil" comes from a Latin word that means "dug up".

Fossils are encased in rock that has to be carefully removed.

This fossil, known as Sue, is the largest, most complete *T. rex* fossil ever found. It was named after Sue Hendrickson, a palaeontologist who discovered it.

Name one difference between fossilization and mummification.

What sort of fossil is that?

There are different types of fossils. Classification depends on how they were created.

Total preservation

This is when the whole animal is preserved, such as an insect in amber.

Semi-preservation

This results when just the hard parts of an object are preserved unaltered.

Petrified

Wood is sometimes petrified. It means the hard parts are preserved, but are chemically altered.

Natural mould

This occurs when the animal or plant decays away, leaving a hole in the rock. The palaeontologist fills this with latex rubber.

Natural cast

This forms as a mould, but the hole is filled by natural substances. For example, a fossil may be cast in a stone called flint.

Trace fossils

These are fossils that show where an animal has been, such as footprints, nests, or coprolites (animal poo).

Picture detective

Look through the Fossils pages to identify each of the picture clues below.

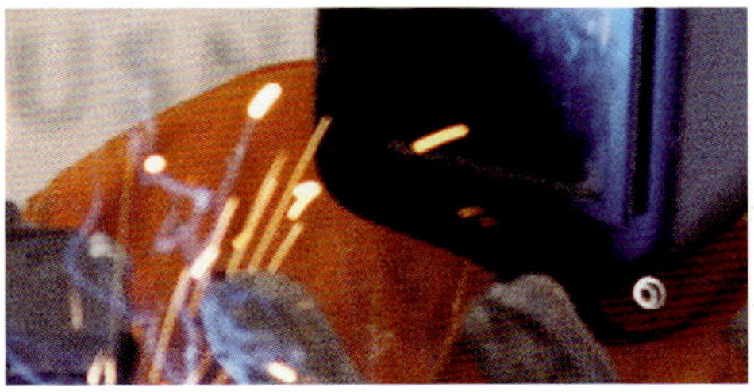

Turn and learn

How a dinosaur may turn into a fossil: **pp. 102–103**

How was it made?

Fossils may form when animal or plant matter is buried, soon after death, under mud or sand. However, that's just the beginning of a process that takes millions of years.

70 million years ago
A *T. rex* has died and is washed downstream. It rests on layers of soft mud and is rapidly buried.

Five years later
The creature's soft flesh has slowly rotted away, leaving the bones. Over time, these begin to move apart.

50 million years ago
A sea has now spread over the area once occupied by the river. Heavy pressure is slowly turning the sand to sandstone.

What are some of the things that fossilize?

Two million years ago

The passing of millions of years has seen mountain ranges rising above the fossilized *T. rex*, but gradually they are being worn down by extreme weather.

Last year

The area around the fossil is now a desert. Two walkers investigate further when they see the exposed tip of a fossilized bone.

Today

Palaeontologists are now hard at work, uncovering the rest of the *T. rex*. The bones will be removed one by one. The skeleton may end up in a museum.

Fossils include bones, teeth, skin impressions, and footprints. Plants also fossilize.

Masses of bones

Certain places are rich in dinosaur fossils. In some areas, dinosaurs may have been drowned in floods; in others, they look like they were caught in traps and many dinosaurs died at about the same time. We can learn a lot from these "dinosaur traps".

A palaeontologist investigates one fossil in a wall of fossils formed when lots of dinosaurs drowned in the same place.

What's been found?

Palaeontologists studied one dinosaur trap in Utah, USA, and discovered more than 10,000 bones. They believe the plant-eaters stopped to drink at a lake, and were trapped in deep mud. Predators were trapped when they approached in the hope of an easy meal.

What we can learn

Fossils can tell us how large an animal was, what it ate, and even how it may have died.

What is a predator?

Ichthyosaur dropping, or coprolite

This one ate fish!

Fossilized droppings can tell us what an animal ate. Ichthyosaurs swam in oceans while dinosaurs ruled the land. This fossilized ichthyosaur dropping has clear fish scales.

What we can't learn

Although dinosaur skin impressions exist, we have no way of knowing what colour dinosaurs really were.

Dinosaur skin impression

Could *T. rex* have been this colourful?

A complete find?

When palaeontologists discover a new dinosaur fossil site, they refer to the bones they find in one of the four ways listed below.

An **articulated** skeleton is a skeleton that is still joined together as it was in life. In rare cases it is almost complete.

An **associated** skeleton is where the bones have broken apart and spread out, but are from the same animal.

Isolated bone is an individual bone that has been separated from the skeleton. It may be a skull or a femur.

Float is what palaeontologists call the scraps of bone that are too small to be of use.

... stuck in mud and die.

After 145 million years, the dinosaur trap is discovered and the fossils exposed.

Investigating a find

It takes an incredibly long time to excavate and examine a fossil find. Sometimes bones are in sand, but usually they have to be removed from rock, which is chipped away in small sections. All the sand and rock has to be removed.

Carefully does it!

If a skeleton is discovered, most of it may be covered with an immense amount of rock and earth, which has to be cleared away. It's a skilful job – nobody wants to damage the fossil.

Palaeontologists investigating the site of a new find

Grid control

It is important that the location and position of the bones are recorded accurately. That's why you'll often see a string grid above a find, so a chart can be mapped.

How might a large fossil be moved once it has its plaster coat?

Don't break it!

At the site, large fossils will be wrapped in bandages and runny plaster. This will set hard to protect the fossil before it can be moved to a museum, where it can be cleaned and examined.

The fossil is wrapped in plaster bandages.

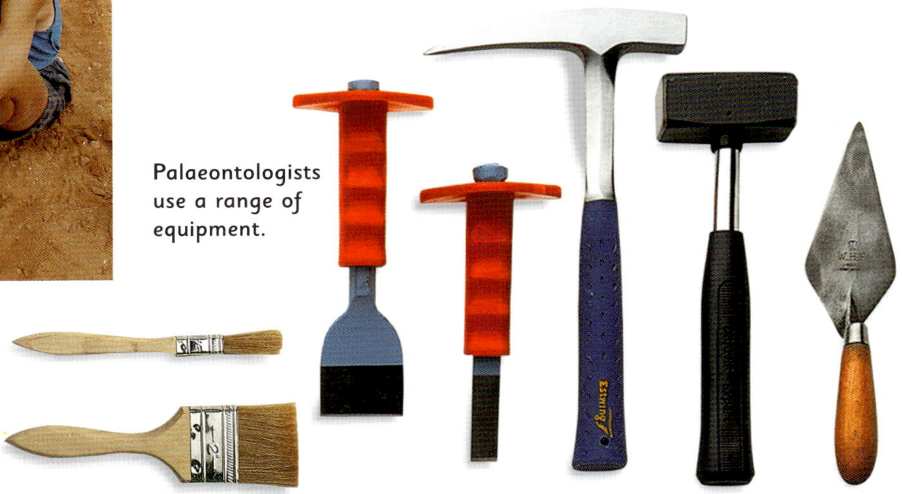

Palaeontologists use a range of equipment.

Paintbrushes are used to remove dust.

Tools of the trade

You'd find a palaeontologist's tool box pretty ordinary, with hammers, trowels, and a range of paintbrushes.

The work doesn't stop

Back at the museum, the plaster cast is removed and the fossil examined. It requires patience. It took technicians more than 3,500 hours (some five months) to clean and repair this one *T. rex* skull. Then a cast was made for exhibition.

Palaeontologists are dinosaur detectives.

A large fossil might be lifted out by a helicopter.

Is it real?

Fossil exhibits in museums are sometimes replicas, as these are lighter in weight and the original fossil can then remain in protective storage. So how is the replica made?

It all begins with the bones

First of all, a mould is made of the fossilized bone. It's done by painting liquid rubber onto the fossil's surface.

The liquid rubber will dry to form a flexible mould.

The next job

Once the rubber has solidified, it is covered in liquid plastic strengthened with fibreglass. This supports the rubber and makes it rigid enough to hold the shape when removed from the bones.

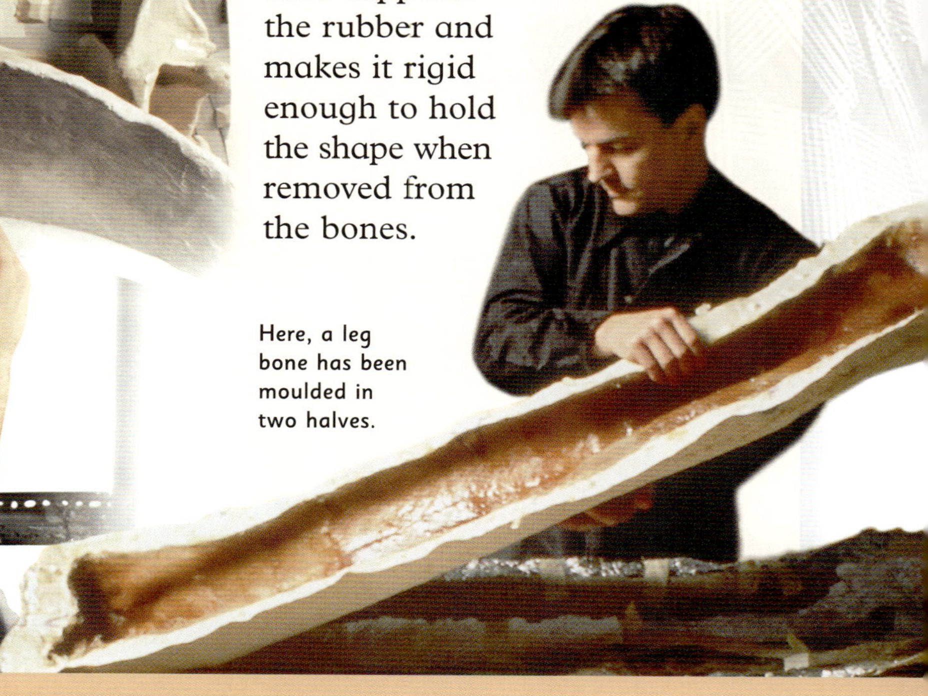

Here, a leg bone has been moulded in two halves.

Can you think of other uses for fibreglass?

Here, an *Allosaurus* model is being put together in a museum exhibit.

Ready to show!

The finished bones are now ready to display. A complete skeleton will be assembled in sections before these sections are brought together. The whole operation takes careful planning.

Turn and learn

Assembling the *Barosaurus* for display: **pp. 110-111**

Filling up the moulds

The shape is then filled with liquid plastic. This will set hard, forming a stiff but lightweight foam. The replica bones need to be light in weight.

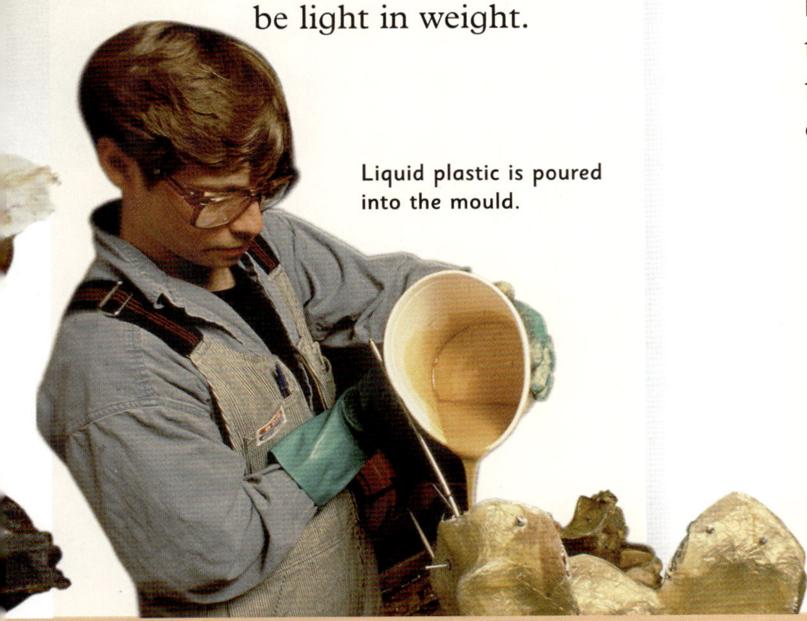

Liquid plastic is poured into the mould.

Let's take a look!

Once the plastic has set, the outer moulds are carefully removed. Any joins are filed to smooth them, and the foam plastic replica bone (cast) will then be painted to match the original fossil.

The cast is easily removed from its mould.

It's a jigsaw

After fossilized bones have been studied and replicas have been made, a museum may decide to mount a display for people to come and see. It can be a long process.

Stick to the plans

There are a lot of bones in a large dinosaur, and specialists have to be careful to get each bone in the right place.

Ready with the ribs

Sometimes parts of the skeleton's frame are assembled elsewhere and then transported to the museum.

Bring in the machines

Some museums are fortunate enough to have high ceilings, perfect for exhibiting a rearing sauropod. This *Barosaurus* skeleton was so large, it needed the help of two cherry-picking machines to position the sections.

When finished, this replica would be more than 15 m (49 ft) high.

How many bones were put together to make the *Barosaurus* skeleton?

Almost done

If a model is enormous, as here, it may need support from metal rods, which have to be welded in position. After all, nobody wants it to fall on a visitor's head!

A welder is protected from sparks by a flame-resistant helmet and gloves.

The finished model shows the mother rearing to protect her young from an approaching *Allosaurus*.

There are more than 200 bones in the *Barosaurus* skeleton.

End of the dinosaurs

The last 10 million years of the Cretaceous period saw a huge variety of dinosaurs. They were flourishing. Yet, the age of dinosaurs was to come to an end.

Who came up with the theory that dinosaurs became extinct because of a meteorite strike?

Why did they die?

There have been many theories about why the giant dinosaurs died out.

Plague wiped out millions in Europe in the 1300s. Did dinosaurs get sick?

Egg predators increased. Did fewer and fewer dinosaur babies survive?

Fire storms, caused by volcanic activity, could have made life harsh.

Tsunami created by earthquakes and meteorites destroyed habitats.

Meteorites from space may have brought widespread devastation.

As **continents shifted**, climate and vegetation changed. Dinosaurs could not adjust to these changes.

Picture detective

Look through the End of the Dinosaurs pages to identify each of the picture clues below.

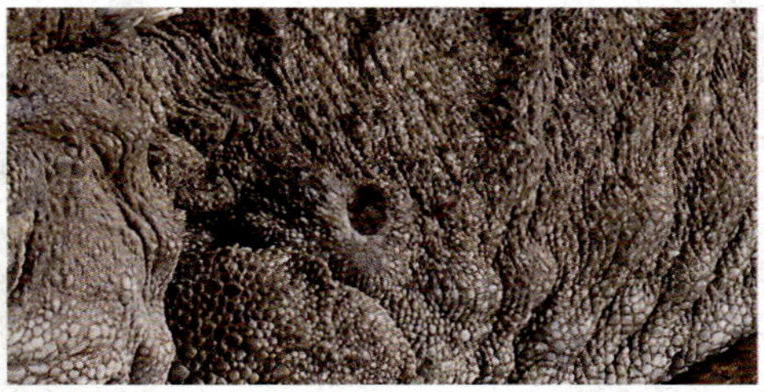

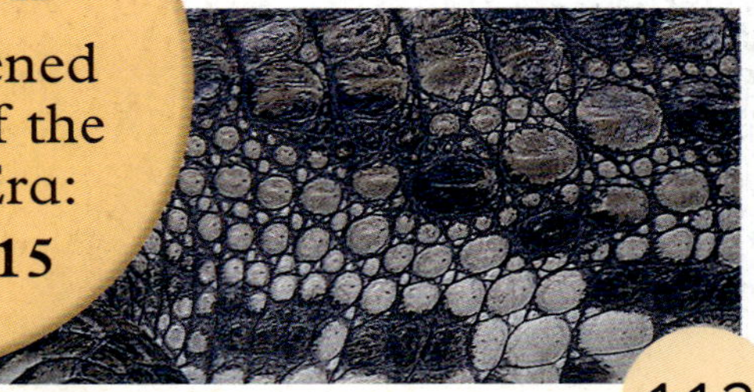

Turn and learn

What happened at the end of the Mesozoic Era: **pp. 114–115**

Nobel laureate Luis Alvarez, and his son, the geologist Walter Alvarez.

What happened?

Sixty-six million years ago, the giant dinosaurs died out, along with the pterosaurs and most marine reptiles. It was a mass extinction, but what caused it? Many believe it was a meteorite.

Who died?

Huge numbers of animals became extinct. Some are listed below.

Pterosaurs had once filled the skies with their airborne acrobatics.

All the different types of **dinosaur** that had evolved died out.

Huge reptiles disappeared from the oceans.

What changed?

Scientists now believe a massive meteorite hit the Earth, creating a dust cloud of noxious fumes that screened out the Sun and changed the climate.

The rock would have hit the Earth's crust with terrific force, sending shock waves around the world.

It was a big one!

In the early 1990s, geologists found the remains of a massive crater in Mexico. It was 180 km (112 miles) wide. They believe it was caused by a meteorite smashing into the Earth 66 million years ago.

How big were the animals that survived the extinction?

Was that all?

The meteorite hit at a time of immense volcanic activity in an area that is now western India. This activity would have sent up clouds of ash and dust that would have blocked the Sun's light – just like the effect of the meteorite hitting the Earth. The extinction may well have been a combination of both these events.

The rock that created the Mexican crater was 10 km (6 miles) in diameter.

An exploding volcano sends up clouds of lethal dust.

No land animal heavier than a large dog survived.

Who survived?

It may have been a catastrophic event for the giant dinosaurs, but incredibly, some creatures did survive the great extinction.

Tiny mammals survived the event that killed off *Triceratops*.

They made it!

Among the animals that survived were sharks, jellyfish, fish, scorpions, birds, and insects.

I was there at the end

Fossil records show us that *Triceratops* was one of the last of the big dinosaurs, along with *T. rex*.

An ancient history

Tuataras – curiously spiny reptiles that live on islands off New Zealand – are related to reptiles that were around at the time of the dinosaurs.

The tuatara survived the extinction!

Which era came after the Mesozoic Era?

Scaly survivors

Although no large land animals made it, a number of smaller reptiles did outlive the dinosaurs.

There are now some 2,900 different types of **snakes**.

Turtles first appeared about 200 million years ago – before the dinosaurs!

There are about 4,500 different **lizards**.

Crocodiles largely inhabit freshwater rivers and lakes.

Flying dinosaurs

Modern birds are now known to be living dinosaurs. Birds of prey use their talons to seize food, just like some giant dinosaurs may have.

The Egyptian vulture is a bird of prey.

Turn and learn
Link between birds and dinosaurs: **pp. 118-119**

Living dinosaurs

You may think that reptiles are closely related to dinosaurs, but dinosaurs may have more in common with birds!

A hidden link?

The link between dinosaurs and birds is clear when you look at *Caudipteryx*, one of the many feathered dinosaurs.

Caudipteryx, a turkey-sized Cretaceous creature, would not have been able to fly as its wings were too small.

The first bird?

The earliest-known bird is *Archaeopteryx*, which first appeared in the Jurassic period. It had the toothed head, clawed fingers, and long bony tail, like that of a dinosaur, but it also had feathers.

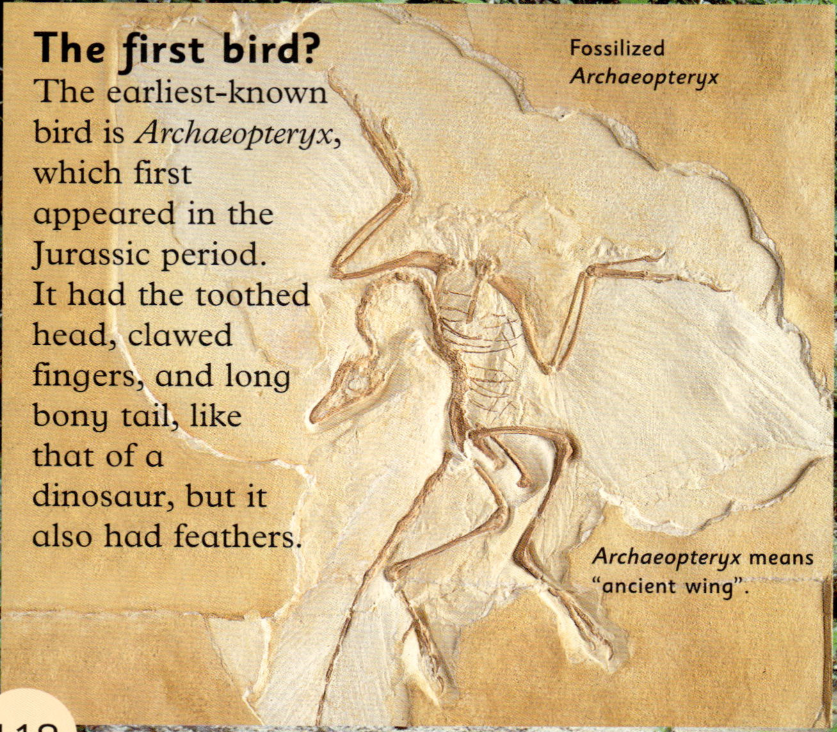

Fossilized *Archaeopteryx*

Archaeopteryx means "ancient wing".

What size did the *Archaeopteryx* reach?

Why feathers?

Feathers protect birds from water and from temperature changes, and they may have served the same purpose on the feathered dinosaurs.

Feathers provide good insulation from cold.

Hoatzin are found in parts of South America.

We have claws

Some modern birds have clawed wings. Hoatzin chicks have two tiny claws at the end of each wing. The adults do not use them, but the chicks do to clamber through trees.

Caudipteryx had clawed hands.

Caudipteryx was about the size of a turkey.

Sinosauropteryx

weird or what?

The evidence that birds are directly descended from dinosaurs is getting stronger all the time. This means that dinosaurs are not extinct! They are living all around us, right now.

Pieces of a puzzle

More and more "dino-birds" are being discovered, and each discovery helps our understanding. This model is based on feathered fossils found in China.

It was small – about the size of a pigeon.

Dinosaur records

The biggest... the smallest... the longest... the tallest... Here are the dinosaur record-breakers!

Fossil of a young *Mussaurus*

As long as a pencil, this young *Mussaurus* lived in the desert lands of Triassic South America. Its name means “mouse lizard”.

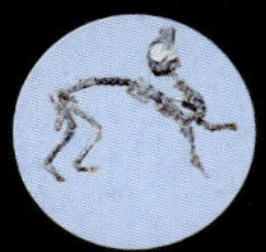

Smallest dinosaur found: A skeleton of a *Mussaurus* was 20 cm (8 in) long – though it was only a baby.

Longest neck: *Mamenchisaurus*’s neck was 14–15 m (46–49 ft) long – about the same as three elephants in a row.

Longest tail: *Diplodocus*’s tail was around 13–14 m (43–46 ft) long.

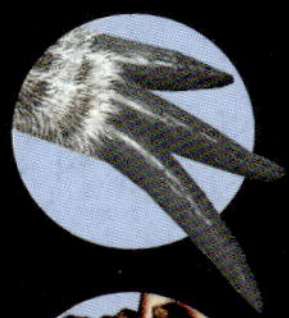

Largest claw: The claws of a *Therizinosaurus* grew to 91 cm (36 in) long – about as long as a man’s arm.

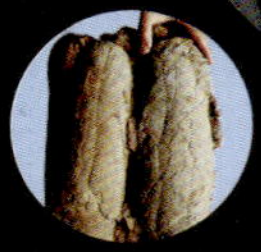

Largest egg: *Macroelongatoolithus xixiaensis* eggs found in China were 46 cm (18 in) long.

Largest head: Both *Pentaceratops* and *Torosaurus* had heads more than 3 m (10 ft) long.

Tallest dinosaur: *Sauroposeidon* stood at a height of 18 m (60 ft) – about as tall as three giraffes standing on top of each other.

Longest dinosaur: *Diplodocus* could reach up to 53.3 m (175 ft).

Biggest meat-eating dinosaur: The 16-m- (52-ft-) long *Spinosaurus* must have been a terrifying predator!

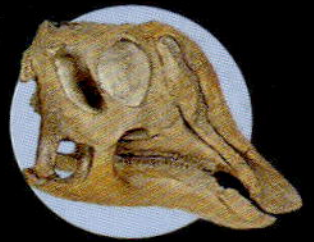

Most teeth: Hadrosaurs, such as *Lambeosaurus*, had more than 1,000 teeth – all for chewing plants!

Smallest adult dinosaur: A fully grown adult *Microraptor* was around 40 cm (16 in) long.

One *Citipati* died on its nest. Some fossil *Citipati* eggs have been found to contain unhatched, fossilized babies.

Will these dinosaur records ever change?

T. rex was among the biggest meat-eaters ever – but it was still smaller than *Spinosaurus*.

Life-size model of *T. rex*

The first *Iguanodon* skeletons were found in Belgium, by coal miners.

Smallest brain: *Stegosaurus* had a brain the size of three table tennis balls.

Fastest dinosaur: It is thought that *Dromiceiomimus* reached speeds of 70 kph (43 mph).

Earliest dinosaur: *Eoraptor* lived about 228 million years ago, in the Triassic period.

First herd found: The first big hoard of dinosaur skeletons was found in 1878. There were 32 skeletons, all of *Iguanodon*.

They might! New dinosaur fossils are being discovered all the time.

True or false?

Can you work out which of these facts are real, and which ones are completely made up?

1 Pterosaurs were flying dinosaurs.

2 Pangaea was a supercontinent in which dinosaurs first lived.

3 Crocodiles are the biggest surviving archosaurs.

4 Caudipteryx, known as a "dino-bird", could fly.

6: False – it had more than 1,000 teeth 7: True 8: False – it means "five-horned face"

5 *Diplodocus* had the longest tail among all dinosaurs.

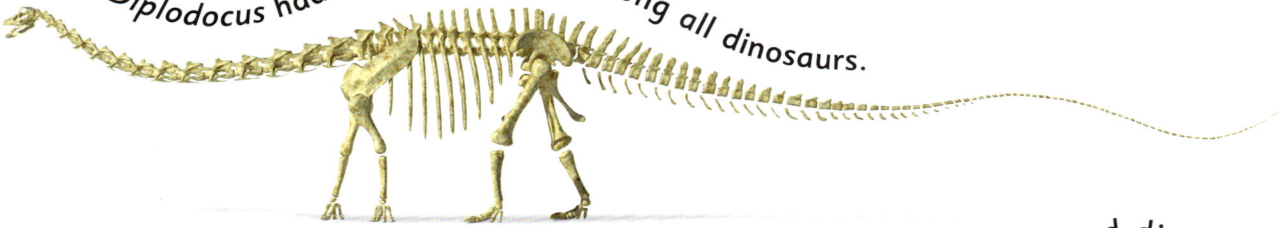

6 A hadrosaur had about 100 teeth.

7 Birds have evolved from lizard-hipped dinosaurs.

8 The name *Pentaceratops* means "three-horned face".

Answers: 1: False – they were flying reptiles 2: True 3: True 4: False – its wings were too small 5: True

Quiz

Test your knowledge of dinosaurs with these quiz questions.

1 Where were the remains of *Iguanodon* first found?

A: France **B: India**
C: Belgium **D: South Africa**

2 Which was the first sauropod to be found?

A: *Megalosaurus* **B: *Cetiosaurus***
C: *Allosaurus* **D: *Eustreptospondylus***

3 Where can you find the tuatara, a relative of the reptiles that existed alongside the dinosaurs?

A: Islands off New Zealand **B: Gobi Desert**
C: Okavango Delta **D: Ghost Ranch**

4 The largest dinosaur egg was laid by...

A: *Macroelongatoolithus* **B: *Citipati***
C: *Therizinosaurus* **D: *Parasaurolophus***

5 What is the nickname of the world's largest and most complete *T. rex* skeleton?

A: Sara **B: Joan**
C: Sue **D: Lucy**

6 Which of these was the earliest-known bird?

A: *Caudipteryx* **B: *Sinosauropteryx***
C: *Archaeopteryx* **D: *Quetzalcoatlus***

7 Which dinosaur is also known as a "living tank"?

A. *Triceratops* **C. *Stegosaurus***
B. *Edmontonia* **D. *Ankylosaurus***

8 Which of these was one of the first marsupials?

A: *Mononykus* **B: *Docodon***
C: *Archelon* **D: *Alphadon***

Pigeon

3: I was eaten by the *Ichthyosaurus*.

Gingko

Squid

Rabbit

Quetzalcoatlus

Poppy

Pansy

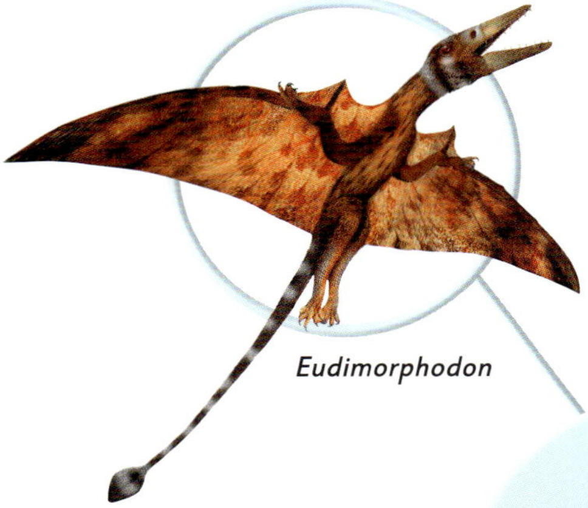
Eudimorphodon

5: I am believed to have been the largest flying reptile of all time.

Rhamphorhynchus

4: I am one of the first flowering plants, appearing in the Cretaceous period.

Pteranodon

Answers. 1: Turtle fossil 2: *Dilophosaurus* 3: Squid 4: Magnolia 5: *Quetzalcoatlus*

1: This dinosaur had about 120 teeth, and its nests have been found in Montana, USA.

6: This was the first sauropod to be found. It lived by an ancient sea in an area now known as England.

2: This place in Arizona, North America, is packed with late Triassic fossils of plants and animals.

3: Fossils of hundreds of dinosaurs were found in this fossil quarry in New Mexico.

4: The near-complete skeleton of this dinosaur was found in 1988 near the Andes mountains.

5: This massive dinosaur lived in the warm swamps of Cretaceous Argentina.

Where in the world?

Discover where the dinosaurs used to roam by matching the descriptions with the pictures.

Cetiosaurus

Ghost Ranch

Velociraptor skeleton

Vulcanodon

Gobi Desert

Yangchuanosaurus

7: *Velociraptor* 8: Gobi Desert 9: *Yangchuanosaurus* 10: *Dryosaurus* 11: *Vulcanodon* 12: *Mamenchisaurus*

7: The bones of this dog-sized dinosaur have been found in Asia.

8: This place is littered with the remains of the sheep-sized *Protoceratops*.

10: This dinosaur from eastern Africa had a parrot-like beak and leaf-shaped teeth.

9: This dinosaur, with the head the size of an armchair, hunted in Jurassic China.

11: This 6.5-m (21-ft) sauropod prowled Jurassic Zimbabwe.

12: This dinosaur was found in Australia, and is the longest-necked animal known to date.

Troodon *Mamenchisaurus* *Herrerasaurus* skeleton *Giganotosaurus* Petrified Forest *Dryosaurus*

Answers: 1: *Troodon* 2: Petrified Forest 3: Ghost Ranch 4: *Herrerasaurus* 5: *Giganotosaurus* 6: *Cetiosaurus*

Glossary

archosaurs One of the group of animals that includes, or included, dinosaurs, birds, pterosaurs, and crocodiles

articulated Things that are joined together, such as the bones of a skeleton

cold-blooded Animal that cannot maintain its body temperature, and has to rely on the Sun's heat to warm up, or find shade in which to cool down. Reptiles are cold-blooded

geologist Scientist who studies the earth and its rocks

habitat Place in which a group of animals and plants live. It could be a desert or a city park

herbivore Animal that only feeds on plants

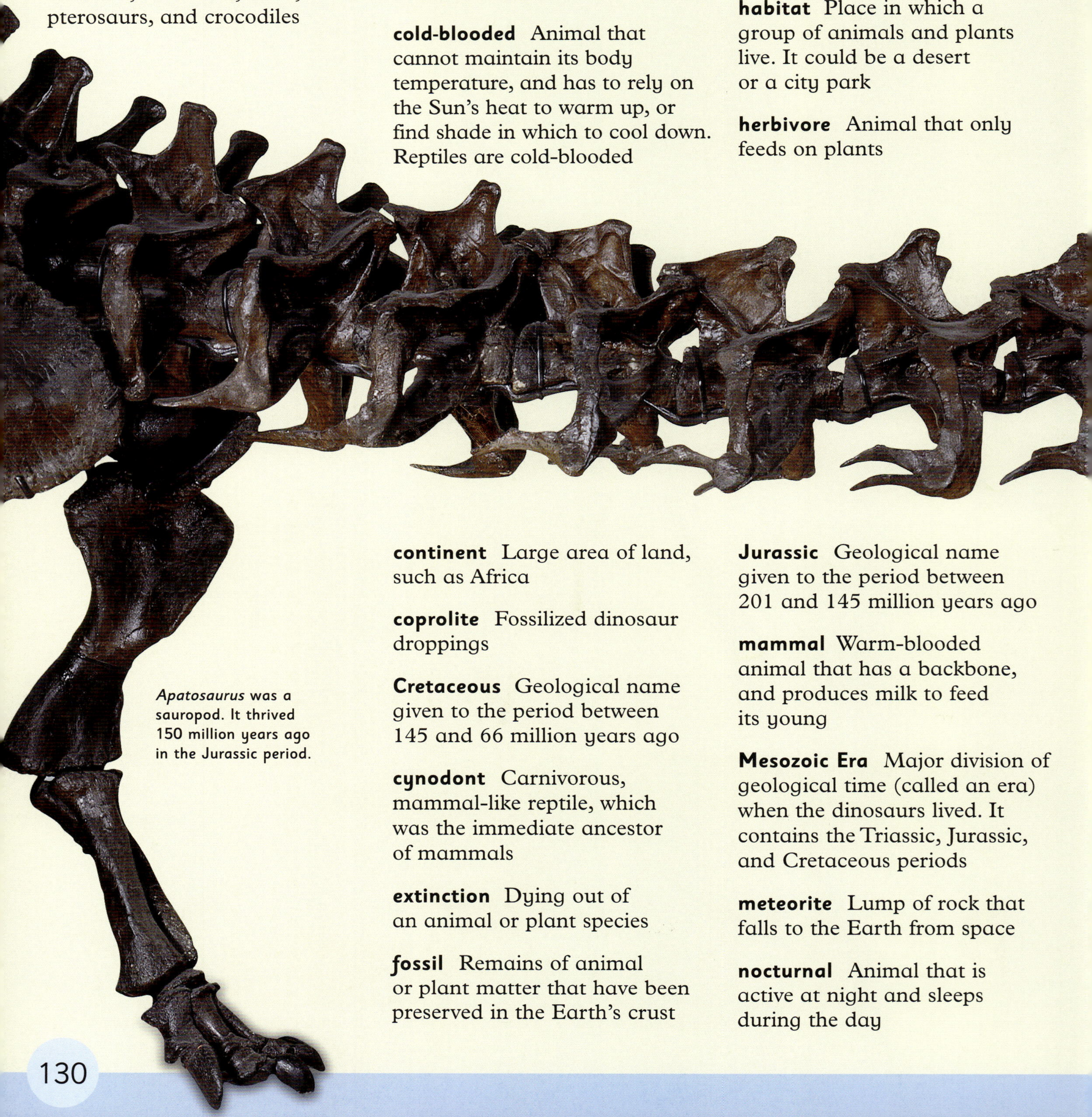

Apatosaurus was a sauropod. It thrived 150 million years ago in the Jurassic period.

continent Large area of land, such as Africa

coprolite Fossilized dinosaur droppings

Cretaceous Geological name given to the period between 145 and 66 million years ago

cynodont Carnivorous, mammal-like reptile, which was the immediate ancestor of mammals

extinction Dying out of an animal or plant species

fossil Remains of animal or plant matter that have been preserved in the Earth's crust

Jurassic Geological name given to the period between 201 and 145 million years ago

mammal Warm-blooded animal that has a backbone, and produces milk to feed its young

Mesozoic Era Major division of geological time (called an era) when the dinosaurs lived. It contains the Triassic, Jurassic, and Cretaceous periods

meteorite Lump of rock that falls to the Earth from space

nocturnal Animal that is active at night and sleeps during the day

palaeontologist Scientist who removes animal and plant fossils from the ground and studies them

predator Animal that hunts and kills other animals for food

prey Animal that is hunted and eaten by another animal

theropod Group name for meat-eating dinosaurs

trace fossil Fossil that indicates where an animal has been, but is not part of the animal's remains. Fossilized footprints are trace fossils

Triassic Geological name given to the period between 252 and 201 million years ago

tsunami Huge wave caused by movements in the Earth's crust. The cause, for example, may be a deep-sea earthquake

warm-blooded Animal that can maintain its body temperature by using food as fuel to generate heat. Humans are warm-blooded

vertebra One of the bones that link together to form an animal's backbone, or spine

reptile One of the group of animals that includes turtles, lizards, crocodiles, snakes, pterosaurs, and dinosaurs

sauropod Name for a group of large, plant-eating dinosaurs. Sauropods had long necks and tails, and bulky bodies

scavenger Animal that feeds on the dead bodies of other animals

species Group of those living things that share the same characteristics, and breed with others of the same type

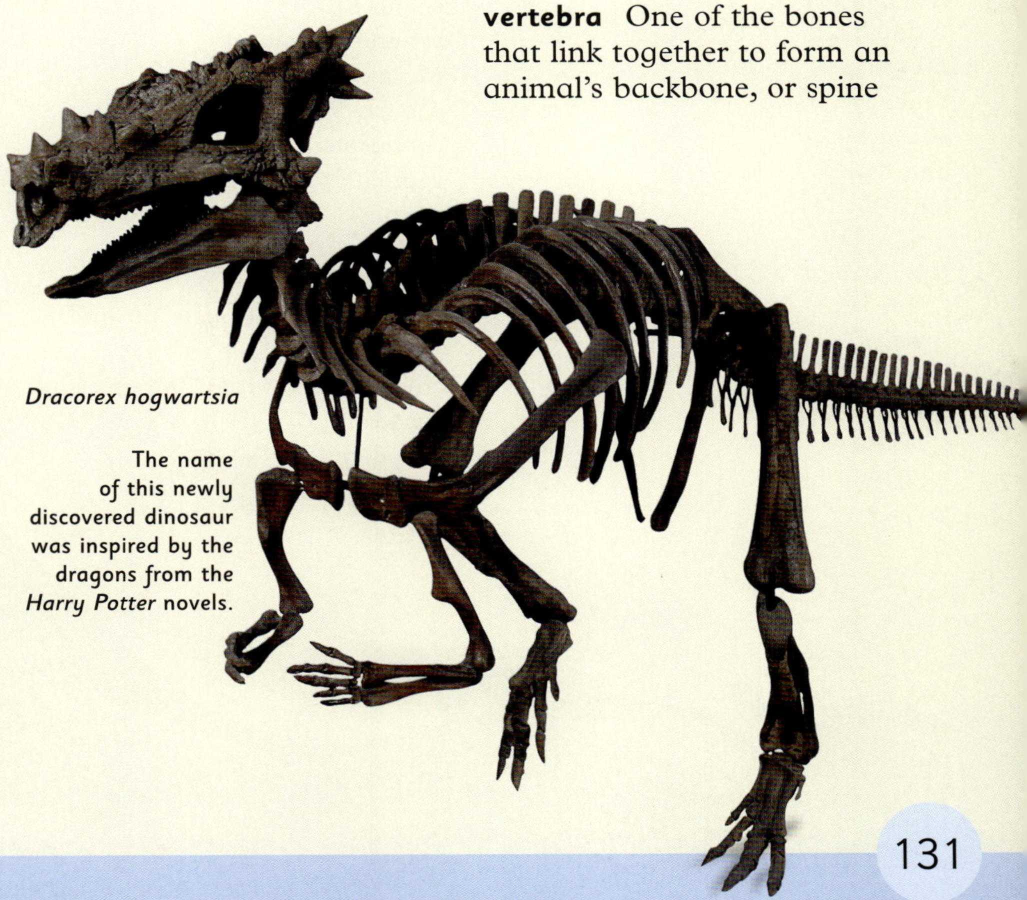

Dracorex hogwartsia

The name of this newly discovered dinosaur was inspired by the dragons from the *Harry Potter* novels.

Index

Can you recognize and name any of the dinosaur silhouettes? Turn to the next page to check your answers.

How many dinosaurs on the previous page did you manage to name?

Spinosaurus
Lesothosaurus
Iguanodon
Protoceratops
T. rex
Euoplocephalus

Picture credits

The publisher would like to thank the following for their kind permission to reproduce their photographs:

(Key: a-above; b-below/bottom; c-centre; l-left; r-right; t-top)

Alamy Images: Jeff Morgan 72b; Werner Otto 126b, 127b; **American Museum Of Natural History**: 47c, 87tl; **Ardea**: Francois Gohier 22br, 58cr, 59cr; **Corbis**: Macduff Everton 129br; Reuters 124cra; Michael S. Yamashita 125cla; Gary Bell 90-91c; Bettmann 46tl; Jonathan Blair 33tr, 36-37bc; Gary Braasch 80-81cb; James D'Addio / Beateworks 10tr; Terry W. Eggers 37crb; Sandy Felsenthal 1bl; Darrell Gulin 14tc; Wolfgang Kaehler 80cl; Layne Kennedy 76cl, 107clb; Macduff Everton 47tl; Charles Mauzy 46ca; Richard T. Nowitz 106cb; Greg Probst 66-67b; Louie Psihoyos 22cl, 22cr, 26tr, 39br, 41tl, 67cra, 68tr, 77tr; Reuters 77br; Reuters / Peter Morgan 54cr; ML Sinibaldi 62-63c (background); Jon Sparks 38tr; Jim Zuckerman 51tr; **DK Images**: American Museum of Natural History 20fcra, 21ca; Angus Beare 113cl; Simone Boni/L.R. Galante 70fcl; Centaur Studios 7fbr, 12fcla, 20tc; Centaur Studios/Andy Crawford 126fbr; Peter Chadwick 35fbr, 84fbl, 85br; Jim Channell 120ftr; Brian Cosgrove 37tc; Bedrock Studios 4bl, 5bl, 19fcr, 39fcl, 57tc, 57bl, 78fbl, 120fcrb, 126fbl; Courtesy of Dinosaur State Park, Connecticut 101fbl; Courtesy of the |Natural History Museum, London 6868fcl; Courtesy of the American Museum of Natural History 68fcl, 73fcrb, 108ftr, 108fbl, 108fbr, 109fbl, 109fbr, 110ftr, 110fclb, 111fcra, 111fcl; Courtesy of the Carnegie Museum of Natural History, Pittsburgh 123fcl; Courtesy of the Field Museum, Chicago 65bc; Courtesy of the Institute of Geology and Palaeontology, Tubingen, Germany 39fcr; Courtesy of the Museo Arentino De Cirendas Naterales, Buenos Aires 75ca; Courtesy of The National Birds of Prey Centre, Gloucestershire 113fcrb, 117fcr; Courtesy of the National Museum of Natural History, Smithsonian Institution 57ftl; Courtesy of the Natural History Museum, London 11bl, 13fcrb, 15fcr, 113cla, 119cla, 120fcr; Courtesy of the Natural History Museum, London / Colin Keates 15c, 18fcl, 21cla; Courtesy of Peter Minister, Digital Sculptor 4-5c, 15crb, 28fcl, 69cl, 75cl; Courtesy of the Royal Tyrell Museum 13fbr; Courtesy of the Royal Tyrrell Museum of Palaeontology, Alberta 65fcr; Courtesy of the Royal Tyrrell Museum of Palaeontology, Alberta, Canada 75fcr, 120fclb; Courtesy of The Sedgewick Museum of Geology, Cambridge 101fcl; Courtesy of the Senckenberg Nature Museum, Frankfurt 65br, 118bl; Courtesy of the State Museum of Nature, Stuttgart 33fcrb, 65fcrb, 105fcra; James Stevenson 19br; Roby Braun 4fbr, 12cb, 17fcr, 17ftr, 73cl, 121cr, 126bc, 126br, 127fbl; Courtsey of Royal Tyrell Museum 69fclb; Andy Crawford 16, 39cla; Dave King 20tl, 120fcra; David Donkin 9bl, 9br; Donks Models 11ftr; Christine M. Douglas 45ftr, 57fbr; Philip Dowell 10fbl, 10bl, 22bl; Mike Dunning 11fcrb; Neil Fletcher / Matthew Ward 57fcra; Giuliano Fornari 114cra, 114crb; Christopher & Sally Gable 25bc; Steve Gorton 57fcrb; Steve Gorton / John Holmes 74cb, 75clb; Jonathan Hateley 27fcl, 113fcra, 118cr, 119clb; Nigel Hicks 11fbr; Graham High, Centaur Studios 4br, 5fbl, 12c, 29bc, 68bc, 69bc, 114cr, 126crb, 127bl, 127br; John Holmes 25ftl, 29fcr; Jon Hughes 34-35b, 35tl, 43tr, 44-45c, 53cr, 56c, 57b, 60c, 61r, 63c, 79cr, 88-89c; Jeremy Hunt 95fcr; Colin Keates 101cla, 101cb; Colin Keates / Courtesy of The Natural History Museum, London 31fcr, 31fcrb, 54cra, 56ftr; Colin Keates / Natural History Museum, London 17fcrb; Gary Kevin 24fcrb, 25fcrb; Gunter Marx 113clb; Ray Moller 10fcl; Frank Greenaway 11br, 14, 95ftr, 95fcrb, 116ca, 116c, 116cb; Natural History Museum, London 24fbl, 29fbr, 31fcra; Stepehen Oliver 99br; Gary Ombler 4bc, 20tr, 27fbl, 63cra, 71crb, 79fcl, 99fcra, 119cb, 127fbr; Gary Ombler; Lloyd Park 59tc, 117fbl; Peabody Museum of Natural History, Yale University 84fclb, 85tc; Peabody Museum of Natural History, Yale University / Lynton Gardiner 84bl; David Peart 116fcl; Miguel Periera 45bc; Roger Phillips 38fbl, 43fcra; Luis Rey 84tl, 84ftl; Rough guides 15ftr, 127c; Karl Shone 113fcr, 116fbl; Steve Shott 95fcra; Staab Studios 120fbr; John Temperton 55fcra, 56fcra, 121crb; Cecile Treal & Jean-Michel Ruiz 11fcr; Matthew Ward 32fcla, 41ftr, 53fcrb; Laura Wickenden 117ftl; James Young 71ftr; Jerry Young 11cr (Scrubland), 14cl, 20cra, 113fbr, 117fclb; **Dorling Kindersley**: Peter Minister 1c; American Museum of Natural History 125bl; Bedrock Studios 129bc (Giganotosaurus), 129fbr; Roby Braun 122ca; Neil Fletcher 127tl; Jon Hughes 124crb, 127cr, 127bc, 128br, 128fbr, 129bl; Instituto Fundacion Miguel Lillo, Argentina 129bc; **Dreamstime.com:** Leonello Calvetti 123t, Christineg 128br (Desert); **FLPA**: Flip de Nooyer / Foto Natura 119tr, 119tc; **Fotolia:** Michael Rosskothen 120crb; **Getty Images**: 77c; AFP / William West 61tl; Theo Allofs 60-61cb (background); Jack Dvkinga 34bc; Rich Frishman 107br; David Hiser 64bl; Brian Kenney 21clb; Raimund Koch 38tl (Background); Timothy Laman / National Geographic 27ca; Klaus Nigge 78-79c (background); Panoramic Images 42l, 43cr, 55c, 68-69bc; Louie Psihoyos 105tl, 105crb, 106cra, 107tl, 120cr, 121c; James Randklev 40-41t; Scott Sady 28-29tc; Miguel Salmeron 26-27bc; Science Faction / Louie Psihoyos 64, 100b, 103t; Pankai & Insy Shah 26-27 (wadi); Andreas Stirnberg 48-49c; Hans Strand 82l, 83br; Steffen Thalemann 44-45b; Nobumichi Tamura / Stocktrek Images 128fbl; **Karen Carr**: 35br; **Kokoro Dinosaurs**: 2-3, 119br, 120bc; **The Natural History Museum, London**: 5br, 6tl, 6cl, 6-7bc, 13crb, 18br, 19cb, 20cr, 21cl, 23bc, 24cl, 25cra, 27tl, 32bl, 67br, 83tl, 88tr, 89c, 120clb, 120cl, 120cla, 120fbl; Anness Publishing 120fcla, 120fcl; De Agostini 54tr; **NHPA / Photoshot**: Andrea & Antonella Ferrari 70-71cb; Jonathan & Angela Scott 34clb; **OSF / photolibrary**: 88cl; Highlights for Children 40bl, 45tc, 45tr; **Reuters**: Peter Morgan 97tc; Ho New 97cra; **Science Faction Images**: Louie Psihoyos 13cra, 18bl, 22cl (background), 23cr, 23tl, 24cra, 31tl, 42clb, 50-51bc, 53tl, 67cr, 79bl, 84-85c, 98cl; **Science Photo Library**: Hervé Conge, ISM 69tl, 126cra; Christian Darkin 8c, 13cla, 30tr, 30-31c, 73t, 97cla; Bernhard Edmaier 115cr; Carlos Goldin 78tr; Gary Hincks 36-37ca; NASA 114bc; Laurie O'Keefe 50clb; David Parker 76-77c; D. Van Ravenswaay 114clb; Joe Tucciarone 86cr; **Mineo Shiraishi**: 53c, 81b; **Still Pictures**: Kelvin Aitken 86l; John Cancalosi / Peter Arnold. Inc. 1cl, 23tc; **SuperStock**: J. Silver 21br; **The Children's Museum of Indianapolis**: 123br; CM Studio: 1r, 34cl, 36tl, 42-43c, 55cr, 57cra, 59tr, 81tr, 126bl, 128; **Tom Dempsey / www.photoseek.com**: 48-49t; **US Geological Survey Western Region**: 11cl; **Special Collections Department**, J. **Willard Marriott Library, University of Utah**: 65tl; **Warren Photographic**: 32-33, 72t, 112-113c, 116tr; Jane Burton 94bc; **Kevin Wasden (kevinwasden.com)**: 53cb; **Yale University Peabody Museum Of Natural History**: 99tl

Additional photography by Andy Crawford: 71ct, 82-83 (*Troodon models*), 88tc, 89tr, 105tl

Acknowledgements

Dorling Kindersley would like to thank:
Tim Batty, The Dinosaur Museum, Dorchester, (www.thedinosaurmuseum.com) for all his help, Penny Smith, Fleur Star, Lorrie Mack, and Carrie Love for editorial assistance and Gemma Fletcher and Hedi Gutt for design assistance. Thank you also to Dougal Dixon for his patience and for allowing photography of his models of Troodon.

Eoraptor, a turkey-sized dinosaur that lived in the Triassic period